Isfahan: Pearl of Persia

Isfahan

Pearl of Persia

TEXT BY WILFRID BLUNT   PHOTOGRAPHS BY WIM SWAAN

Elek Books Limited, 54-58 Caledonian Road, London N1 9RN

I.G.D.A., Officine Grafiche, Novara - 1974
Printed in Italy

Contents

List of illustrations

Illustrations in the text

Jacket illustration:
front: Minarets of the College of the Mother of the Shah
back: *Haftrangi* tile-work

Front endpaper:
Mosaic tile-work from the Friday Mosque

Back endpaper:
Mosaic tile-work from the dome of the Lutfullah Mosque

Title page:
Papier mâché box dated 1848, showing the Governor of Isfahan holding court.

Acknowledgments

The author and publishers express their gratitude to Mr Ralph Pinder Wilson, for his help in checking the manuscript of this book, and to the following for permission to use illustrations from works of which they hold the copyright:

Librairie Hachette (for Figs. 5, 6, 7, 8, 11, 13, 14, 15, 17, 18, 19, 20, 21, 23).

Oxford University Press (for Figs. 3, 4).

Thanks are also due to the following for kindly supplying photographs: British Museum (for Plates 39, 79, 80, 81, 82, 83, 84, 85, 86, 87, 88, 89, 90, 91); Victoria and Albert Museum (for Plates 35, 36, 41, 53, 64, 71, 72).
Plates 2, 4, 5, 12, 15, 16, 17, 19, 32, 55, 56 and 69 are from photographs by Wilfrid Blunt; all other photographs in this volume are by Wim Swaan.

Introduction

IT IS SCARCELY an exaggeration to say that Isfahan is the creation of a single man —Shah Abbas the Great.

It is true that one of its finest buildings, the Friday Mosque, was for the most part constructed some centuries before he came to the throne in 1587; it is true also that his immediate successors continued to embellish the city: but all that is most characteristic of Isfahan today, bears the stamp of his personality. Isfahan is Shah Abbas's memorial: *Si monumentum requiris, circumspice.*

The traveller, if he approaches Isfahan by road, must traverse, from whatever direction he comes, many miles of tawny, desolate plain and bleak stony uplands. Flowers, except at the brief burgeoning of spring, are scarce and undramatic; there are few villages and little to enliven the journey. Thus the sudden, still distant prospect of Isfahan comes like a drink of water to a thirsty man. It comes with the flash of a shimmering blue dome, of minarets and further domes rising above a swarm of lesser buildings and outlying gardens and scattered pigeon-towers.

If the traveller approaches the city from Tehran he will enter it by one of the newly-constructed *khiabans* (avenues); if he comes from Shiraz, he will cross the Zayandeh-rud (Zayandeh river) by the Thirty-three-arch bridge and enter the Chahar Bagh Avenue—both the creation of Abbas. On the way to his hotel—whichever that may be—he will not, however, immediately pass the Maidan, the great Square that is the focal point of the city, but this will inevitably be his first objective when he sets out to view the town.

No one, however much he may have read of Isfahan, whatever he may have studied in photograph or in painting, can escape a gasp of astonishment at the first sight of the Maidan—a square seven times the size of the Piazza di San Marco in Venice and more than twice as large as Moscow's Red Square. It is huge, and at its northern end not as yet very *soigné*; but elsewhere a municipal hand has transformed the great open space where polo was once played, converting it into a pleasant but conventional western-style garden. None the less, the Maidan remains unlike any other square in the world.

At the southern end of the Maidan stands the Masjid-i-Shah or Royal Mosque, its vast *ivan* (portal) surmounted by two lofty minarets and dominated by a massive blue dome. To the east is the Shaikh Lutfullah Mosque with its glittering entrance and squat buff and turquoise dome. To the west the Ali Qapu, a columned grandstand, enchanting and yet slightly absurd, forms the gateway to what was once the Palace grounds; from its shady balcony Shah Abbas and his courtiers used to watch the pageantry and the polo taking place below. To the north where life is most teeming, is the entrance to the main Bazaars. For the rest the Maidan is bounded by a simple white wall, arcaded and two storeys tall, picked out in the blue that is the very soul of Iran[1]. To spend an hour in the Maidan and the buildings that abut on it is to get closer to Persia than by reading a hundred books.

But Isfahan is more than the Maidan and its royal buildings. There are splendid bridges. There is still the ghost of the Chahar Bagh, Shah Abbas's broad avenue that cuts through the city and crosses the Zayandeh-rud to Julfa, his Armenian settlement. And everywhere there are lesser mosques, some of which have tile-work of astonishing beauty. Isfahan is a city with which it is not difficult to fall in love. The architecture of Meshed may be purer; Shiraz may be more up-to-date; life in Tehran may be more sophisticated: but Isfahan is the quintessence of Iran. ' *Isfahan nisf-i-Jahan*,' wrote a Persian poet: ' Isfahan is half the world.'

Fig. 1. The Chihil Sutun: detail of column bases.

Iran   Part 1

THE WESTERN READER who opens a book on Venice, Paris or one of the other great cities of Europe will already be armed with at least a working knowledge of the historical background against which the scene is set. There will be no need to remind him that Louis XIV ruled over France in the second half of the seventeenth century, or to explain that Raphael was an Italian painter. Terms such as ' Protestant ', ' Doge ', ' the French Revolution ', ' the Thirty Years' War ' or ' the Acropolis '—to take a mere handful at random—convey an instant meaning. He may not, however, be equally familiar with their equivalents in an Islamic country in the Middle East. He knows about the Bourbons but not about the Safavids, about Calvinism but not about Shi'a and Sunni; he knows that Holland is flat and Switzerland mountainous, but very probably he has little notion of the physical aspects of Iran. It will therefore be necessary, before discussing Isfahan in detail, to provide him with a thumbnail sketch of the country of Iran, its people and its history, and to supplement this with a synopsis of the rise and fall of Isfahan itself.

The Persians have often been called the French of the Middle East: in many respects it would be more accurate to compare them to the Spaniards, and at all events no one would deny the great similarity of the physical aspects of Spain and Iran. Both countries contain a vast central tableland, arid in summer and often bitterly cold in winter. Both have wild mountainous areas, tawny and infertile. But in Iran the contrasts are greater, the scale larger, the colours more violent, the mountains loftier, the extremes of heat and cold more pronounced. It was Cyrus the Great who once commented that at one end of his kingdom his subjects might be dying of cold while at the other end they were being suffocated by the intense heat.

To both countries, too, came Islam. Though Spain in due course shook herself free of the invaders and rejected their creed, their occupation left a permanent mark, not only on the style of her architecture but also on the character of her people. The Spaniard and the Iranian are both proud, both hospitable, both procrastinating: the *mañana* of the Spaniard may not have its exact equivalent in current use in Iran today, but the spirit of *farda* (tomorrow) still prevails there. Buses leave *farda* or *pasfarda* (the day after tomorrow), rarely *emruz* (today), as every traveller in the country knows to his cost. Yet it is this leisureliness, this readiness to let tomorrow take care of itself, that is one of the great charms of Iran after the turmoil and restlessness of the modern Western world.

> Unborn TOMORROW, and dead YESTERDAY,
> Why fret about them if TODAY be sweet!

But whereas Spain lies at the extremity of a continent, Iran is situated in the heart of Asia. She was so placed that the great trade caravans passing between Cathay and the West inevitably crossed her northern territories, bringing her the wealth that falls to the middle-man. She became, quite effortlessly, the emporium of the Middle East. From the Indies, Tartary and Cathay came pearls and precious stones, silks and spices, cochineal and rhubarb, Kashmir shawls and Indian indigo; from Europe came velvets and watered silks, coral and amber, glassware and iron, lace and gold thread.

Then in 1497 Vasco da Gama rounded the Cape and opened up sea communications with India. This brought maritime trade to the ports on the Persian Gulf, but conflict with Portugal to whom fell the lion's share of the profits; it was the first blow struck at the age-old overland routes, which were to receive their *coup de grâce* when, nearly four hundred years later, the construction of the Suez Canal more than halved the sea journey from Europe to the Further East.

What we have long known as 'Persia' has now again become 'Iran'. The words 'Iran' and 'Aryan' have a common origin. The Medes were the first Aryan peoples to gain ascendancy in Persia, which they began to occupy in the eighth century B. C. Two centuries later the Persians, a nomadic Aryan tribe, also settled in the country. In 550 B. C. the Persians, under Cyrus the Great, subdued the Medes, overran practically the whole of the then known world, and founded the Achaemenid dynasty. The ruins of the great ceremonial palaces of Persepolis, near Shiraz, still testify to the splendour of the Persian empire under Darius (521-485 B. C.) and his successor, Xerxes.

But the days of Achaemenid rule were numbered. In 333 B. C. the Greeks, under Alexander the Great, defeated the Persians at the Battle of Issus, and again two years later at Arbela, and so brought the dynasty to a close. After the death of Alexander, Seleucus, one of his generals, formed a dynasty which endured for a century. The Seleucids were followed by the Parthians (223 B. C. – A. D. 226), nomads from the north-eastern steppes. They maintained an empire strong enough to defeat the Romans and to hold the Scythian invaders at bay.

It was the rise of a powerful national dynasty in Fars, the province that had been the home of the Achaemenids, which finally brought about the downfall of the Parthians. The Sasanians (A. D. 226-658), as they were called, founded an empire that was more than a match, on several occasions, for Rome and Byzantium; their remarkable rock carvings at Shapur, Naqsh-i-Rostam and elsewhere in Iran, and some fine repoussé silverware, still survive as evidence of their artistic ability.

The most important event in Iranian history was, of course, the conquest of the country by the Arabs under the Caliph Omar, who in 642 introduced the religion of Islam. The Seljuq Turks, from the Central Asian steppes, ruled Iran from 1037 to 1187. In the thirteenth century came the Mongol invasions under Chingiz Khan and Hulagu Khan, to be followed a century later by the even greater scourge of Tamerlane. But if the Mongols destroyed, they also built—and built splendidly. Tamerlane's descendants, the Timurids (1380-1499), also encouraged the arts; many of their buildings still stand, and their illuminated manuscripts have never been surpassed.

It was under the Timurids' successors, the Safavids (1499-1736), that Isfahan was transformed from a provincial city into one of the greatest capitals in the world of its day.

The first Safavid ruler was a certain Ismail, saint and warrior, who in 1499 seized Tabriz, proclaimed himself Shah, and by further conquests established the first truly native dynasty to govern Iran for nearly a millenium. In 1598, the fifth of the line, Shah Abbas the Great, transferred his capital from Qazvin to Isfahan and so inaugurated a century of unparalleled splendour and prosperity.

Even before the advent of Abbas, Isfahan had been a city of some importance. The great Friday Mosque, dating back at least as early as the eleventh century, is evidence enough of its importance, and this is confirmed by the accounts of a number

I

2

of travellers, including several Italians, who visited the city in pre-Safavid times. None the less, the Isfahan we admire today—the city that in the seventeenth century attracted merchants, adventurers and the idly curious from Europe; the city to which emperors, kings and popes were eager to send ambassadors and envoys—was the creation of Shah Abbas. Palaces, mosques and bridges; a splendid avenue and a magnificent square, sprang up at his command. His government, by contemporary standards, was tolerant and humane, his ideas advanced. The West came to the Persia of Abbas to admire and to learn, not, as was later to be the case, to render aid to an underdeveloped country.

Abbas died in 1629, and the Safavid dynasty struggled on for another century. But the pattern was henceforth one of almost uninterrupted decline. His successors lacked his stature. They drank or they shut themselves up in their harems; they were too dissolute or too pious or too feeble to govern. So the country ran slowly but steadily downhill: we find an almost exact parallel in the later Mughal emperors, the unworthy successors of Akbar the Great.

In the year 1722 the Afghans invaded Persia. Isfahan was taken and the dynasty overthrown; soon after the capital was transferred to Meshed, and Isfahan became once again, and remained, a provincial city.

This book, therefore, is principally concerned with the century that followed upon the accession of Shah Abbas in 1587—the Golden Age of Isfahan. We must, of course, also consider Isfahan's rise to greatness; nor can we ignore its downfall and the era of anarchy that followed, the stagnation that endured throughout the nineteenth century, or the new life that is stirring today.

But Isfahan is Abbas, and Abbas is Isfahan; there is no other great city in the world which owes its greatness so entirely to the genius of a single ruler.

Fig. 2. Detail of tile decoration in the Friday Mosque.

2. Faience recess in the Friday Mosque dated A. D. 1447. The artist's name is given as Sayyid Mahmud.

The early history of Isfahan

SCHOLARS HAVE LONG disputed the origin of the word *Isfahan*. It may be the Aspa-dana of Ptolemy, and there are Sasanian coins showing the letters ASP; it could be derived from *sipahan* or *aspahan*, 'armies'; and there are some, in other parts of Iran, who claim that *asbahan*, a local word for 'dogs', would fittingly describe a town where, as a Persian poet once wrote, 'nothing is lacking but decent people'.

Nor is there certainty as to the date of the town's foundation. The name of the legendary Jamshid is inevitably invoked, but there are reasonably solid grounds for believing that under the Achaemenid kings a city named Gabal or Gavi existed on the site and that it became the Jay of the Sasanians. The first unchallenged date is the year A. D. 643, when, after the Battle of Nihavand, the city fell to Caliph Omar and his irresistible Muslim armies. The feeble Yezdigird III fled to Balkh where he died nine years later, thus bringing the Sasanian dynasty to an end after more than four centuries.

In the tenth century Isfahan was governed by various petty princes, chiefly of Fars and Iraq. One of these, a certain Mardavij, who captured the city in 931, held a great festival there; it has been described, in somewhat fanciful terms, by Sa'id Nafisi in his *Mah-i-Nakhshab*: [2]

> With this in view, Mardavij ordered the people to collect brushwood and fuel from the desert and pile it upon the banks of the river. He brought oil in goatskins over great distances, and ordered the men known as 'oil-throwers', who used to dip wood in oil and after lighting it throw it most skilfully over great distances, to gather there too. He prepared great candles, each as tall as a man, then treated them with camphor and placed them in position. On Garmkuh and all the other hills near the city he heaped up great piles of wood. He brought great trunks of trees and logs from outside the city, bound them together with iron bands in the form of palaces and pulpits, filled them with shavings and brushwood and placed them outside the city boundaries. In addition, hunters collected more than a thousand ravens and kites and bound oily walnut bark, wood and shavings to their beaks and legs.
>
> Then Mardavij gave orders that every hill and valley and the whole wide plain should be lighted simultaneously, and that the whole vast district should sparkle and flame as far as the eye could see. That same evening he spread such a board as the world had never seen, such lavishness, such generosity and such splendour.

At this time Isfahan consisted of two distinct quarters, Yahudiyyeh (Jewish city) and Shahristan ('township', or city proper), lying about two miles apart. Though legend asserts that it was Nebuchadnezzar who had first settled the Jews in Isfahan, they probably arrived in late Sasanian times; Shahristan was presumably the older part of the city and the original Jay.

In a geographical work, *Hudud al-'Alam*, written in the tenth century, the twin cities are described as very flourishing and 'much favoured by nature', and as already producing large quantities of the silk textiles for which Isfahan continued to be famous. Soon after this, Yahudiyyeh and Shahristan were enclosed within a single wall. About the same time began the building of the Citadel, which survived until well into the present century and whose moats still remain.

3. Detail of chiselled stucco-work from the Mihrab of Öljaitu in the Friday Mosque, dated A. D. 1310.

The first comprehensive picture of Isfahan is that given by Nasir-i-Khusrau in his *Safar-Nameh* or 'Book of Travel', composed in the middle of the eleventh century.

4

5

Though the town had recently been besieged and captured by the Seljuq, Tughril
Beg, it appears to have suffered little damage, for Nasir-i-Khusrau wrote: [3]

> The town is situated on a plain. Its climate is agreeable; and wherever one sinks a well to a depth of ten *gaz* [about thirty-six feet], excellent cold water gushes out. It has a strong, high wall with gates and fortifications, and all the walls are battlemented. Inside are channels of running water and tall, handsome buildings, and in the centre of the city stands the great and magnificent Friday Mosque. They say that the town walls are three and a half *farsangs* [over thirteen miles] in length. The city looks uniformly prosperous, and I did not see a single building in ruins. I noticed a large number of bazaars, and in one of these, which was that of the moneychangers, there were two hundred men of this profession. Each bazaar has its wall and its gate, as has every quarter and street. There are clean and well-kept caravanserais... No one noticed our arrival in the city, and there was so much room that we had no difficulty in finding food and lodging. I have never seen, anywhere where Persian is spoken, a finer, larger or more prosperous town than Isfahan.

In this account we have the first mention of the greatest of all the early buildings of Isfahan, the Friday Mosque (Masjid-i-Jami), whose splendours will presently be discussed.

Then came the Mongols, under Chingiz Khan, and later under Tamerlane (Timur-i-lang). In 1228 a great but inconclusive battle was fought outside Isfahan and the city was captured but not destroyed. Ibn Battuta, the Moor of Tangier who travelled from Morocco to India in the fourteenth century, was in Isfahan about 1330, by which time religious wars had seriously damaged the town that the Mongols had so surprisingly spared. He wrote:

> The next day our way lay through orchards and streams and fine villages, with very many pigeon towers, and in the afternoon we reached Isfahan ... Isfahan is one of the largest and fairest of cities, but most of it is now in ruins, as a result of the feud between Sunnis and Shi'ites,[4] which is still raging there. It is rich in fruits, among them being apricots of unequalled quality with sweet almonds in their kernels, quinces whose sweetness and size cannot be paralleled, splendid grapes, and wonderful melons. Its people are good looking, with clear white skins tinged with red, exceedingly brave, generous, and always trying to outdo one another in procuring luxurious viands.
> Many curious stories are told of this last trait in them. The members of each trade form corporations, as also do the leading men who are not engaged in trade, and the young unmarried men; these corporations then engage in mutual rivalry, inviting one another to banquets, in the preparation of which they display all their resources. I was told that one corporation invited another and cooked its viands with lighted candles; then the guests returned the invitation and cooked their viands with silk.[5]

Fifty years later, in the winter of 1386, the hordes of Tamerlane descended upon Isfahan from the north. Camp was pitched outside the town, whose leading citizens were summoned to confer. The stories of Tamerlane's sackings and bloodshed in the north had made them in a mood to meet any reasonable demands; Tamerlane also, anxious to rest his troops, was ready to be conciliatory: for a heavy ransom he would spare the town. The deputation agreed to his terms, and tax-collectors were sent into Isfahan to collect the stipulated money and jewels.

But when the inhabitants found themselves being stripped of their wealth, they rashly rose in revolt: ' Rather death ', they said, ' than this '; and death it was that they chose. During the night, on an agreed signal given by the beating of a drum, the populace attacked and annihilated the tax-collectors, several thousand in number. Then they murdered the guards posted by Tamerlane at the entrances to the city, and closed and barricaded the gates. Tamerlane's awful vengeance may be best told in the splendid oriental hyperbole of Ibn Arabshah, his Arab biographer, who wrote soon after the events that he describes:

> But when dawn had drawn her sword and day had stripped off his covering, Tamerlane perceived that evil crime. And Satan puffed up his nostrils, and forthwith he moved his camp and drew the sword of his wrath and took arrows from the quiver of his tyranny and advanced upon the city, roaring, overthrowing, like a dog or lion or leopard. And when he came in sight of the city

4. The Shahristan Bridge. The piers of the bridge are probably Sasanian, the upper part Seljuq.

5. The Jorjir Portal. It is all that now remains of a tenth-century mosque.

he ordered bloodshed and sacrilege, slaughter and plunder, devastation, burning of crops, women's breasts to be cut off, infants to be destroyed, bodies dismembered, honour to be insulted, dependents to be betrayed and abandoned, the carpet of pity to be folded up and the blanket of revenge to be unfolded. Nor did he pity the aged for his age, or the infant for his infancy, or honour the learned for his learning,[6] or the educated for his excellence, or the noble for his blood, or the eminent for his dignity or the stranger for his strangeness, the kinsman for his kinship and propinquity, or the Moslem for his faith, the dependent for his dependence, the weak for his weakness, the obtuse for the weakness of his judgment and his obtuseness. Altogether he showed no pity to any of the townspeople....[7]

So the massacre continued until the number of the dead was ' six times more than the people of Nineveh '. Then one of the ' wise men ' of Isfahan approached a Mongol *amir* and implored him to use his influence to put a stop to the slaughter. The *amir* replied, ' Collect some infants on the hills, that Tamerlane may be a little softened by the sight of them—as by chance may happen '. This was done, and the *amir*, as he rode by with Tamerlane, begged him to order an end to the massacre. But Tamerlane ' made no reply and uttered no speech, but urged his horse into them, as though he had not seen them ... Then collecting wealth and baggage and placing goods on the baggage animals he returned with booty to Samarqand '.

Behind him, as a fearful warning, Tamerlane left one of his infamous ' towers of skulls ', made from the heads of seventy thousand of the inhabitants—one skull collected, as he had ordered, by each of his seventy thousand soldiers. One authority states that some of Tamerlane's men, unwilling to carry out this cold-blooded murder, preferred to buy heads from their comrades at the rate of a gold piece each. But most were not so squeamish: supply soon exceeded demand, and the price steadily dropped until, such was the pleasure of killing for killing's sake, heads were finally available free of charge. Nevertheless, Tamerlane does not seem to have destroyed any of the principal buildings of Isfahan, and some of those which he spared stand to this day.

Tamerlane ruled from Samarqand, his son and successor Shah Rukh from Herat; thus the western part of their empire was largely left in the hands of the younger princes of the house. By the middle of the fifteenth century the Timurids had lost their grip of most of Iran proper, where events were chiefly concerned with the rivalry of two Turkoman tribes—the Black Sheep, who were established near Lake Van, and the White Sheep, based on Diarbekr. Finally the White Sheep, under Uzun Hasan, were victorious, and their leader made Tabriz his capital.

At this point Venice comes into the picture. Both Uzun Hasan and the Venetians were anxious to check the growing power of the Ottoman Turks, and with this in view Venice sent ambassadors and merchants to Uzun Hasan in Tabriz. It happened that one of these ambassadors, Josafa Barbaro, accompanied Uzun Hasan to Isfahan, and that his successor, Ambrogio Contarini, joined him there in 1474. Both wrote accounts of their travels, in which they briefly described the city and their experiences there.

' Isfahan ', wrote Contarini, ' seems to be a very convenient city, and is situated in a plain abounding with all kinds of provisions. It is said that, as this city refused to surrender, much of it was destroyed after it was captured. It is surrounded by a wall of earth like the others.[8] He found the general cost of living high, but the price of bread reasonable. The people were friendly and seemed to like the Christians: ' while we were in Persia we did not suffer a single outrage '.

Barbaro was chiefly impressed by the innumerable warehouses in which merchants could keep their goods. These were vaulted rooms, locked at night, surrounding a courtyard in the middle of which was a square pool of excellent drinking water.

Contarini describes their reception by Uzun Hasan, who greeted them cordially and made them sit with his lords. Then ' an abundant supply of refreshments was

6. A part of the complex of vaulted chambers in the Friday Mosque, dating from the twelfth to fourteenth centuries.

brought, well prepared, according to their methods, of which we partook, seated on the carpets in the Persian fashion '.

Two days later they were again summoned by Uzun Hasan, who allowed them to inspect his palace, which was pleasantly situated in a meadow beside the river. In one of the courtyards Contarini noticed a painting representing the decapitation of ' Soltan Busech '. After an excellent luncheon they returned to their lodging.

The Ambassadors stayed in Isfahan for three weeks. During this time they were invited to numerous royal banquets at which some 400 guests were usually present. Contarini mentions the great copper vessels in which the food, chiefly rice and corn dishes, was brought in, and remarks that it was a pleasure to see how enthusiastically the guests attacked it. Uzun Hasan drank wine with his meals and clearly enjoyed his food. His private band and some singers performed when he commanded.

Uzun Hasan appeared to be about seventy years old—tall[9] and slim, with a slightly Tartar cast of countenance and a high complexion. He was good company and an excellent host, but dangerous when too deep in his cups. Contarini noticed that his hand trembled when he drank.

Uzun Hasan cross-examined the ambassadors about Venice, and as a result Persian metalworkers were despatched, who settled permanently in the city. Their wonderful interlacing designs spread to Nuremberg and Augsburg, where they were published in books that were widely disseminated. The work of goldsmiths in Elizabethan England shows an unmistakable Persian influence. From a military point of view, however, the projected alliance was a failure. Uzun Hasan waged war vigorously against the Ottoman Empire; but the princes of Christendom, occupied with their own quarrels and rivalries, failed to unite to give him proper support.

The White Sheep dynasty did not survive the fifteenth century: after the death of Uzun Hasan in 1478, intrigues over the succession led to its downfall, and in 1499 a certain Ismail, whose mother was the daughter of Uzun Hasan, seized the reins of government and founded the Safavid dynasty, so inaugurating the most splendid era in the history of Isfahan.

7. Detail of tile mosaic from
the *ivan* leading to the Sanctuary
of the Friday Mosque.
Part of the mosaic can be attributed
to the fourteenth century.

Pre-Safavid architecture

We have traced the history of Isfahan from the earliest times down to the end of the fifteenth century; we must now take stock of the buildings which survive from the pre-Safavid period.

Atashgah

Virtually nothing remains from before the Arab conquest; but on a conical hill about four miles to the west of the city may still be seen the mud-brick ruins of an *atashgah* or Zoroastrian fire-temple dating in origin from Sasanian times.

Zoroastrianism had been the religion of the Persians from the days of the Achaemenids until it was almost extinguished by the persecutions following the Arab invasion in the seventh century. Though it is impossible to suggest a date for the life-span of Zoroaster himself, there seems little doubt that he must be considered as a historic and not a legendary figure. Many classical authors mention him, and Pliny, in his *Natural History*, gives us the improbable information that he laughed on the day of his birth and that he lived in the wilderness upon cheese.

At the time of the Muslim conquest, many Zoroastrians took refuge in Yazd and Kirman, where some have lingered on, ' maltreated ', until the present day. Others, however, left these towns in due course for Bombay where they became known as Parsees and flourished exceedingly. In eastern Iran, the Zoroastrians still expose their dead upon 'towers of silence' to be devoured by birds of prey; their ancient faith survives and persecution is today virtually at an end. In Yazd, the chief stronghold, there are now probably some 7,000 Zoroastrians—or Guebres, as they are called—in a total population of about 66,000. There (as elsewhere in Iran) can be seen a modern Zoroastrian fire-temple where the undying flame burns among tubular metal chairs inscribed with the names of the donors.

Of earlier fire-temples in Iran, little remains today beyond fragments of walls of uncertain date. The *atashgah* outside Isfahan now consists only of a small brick building which is certainly in no part pre-Islamic, and scattered material that may possibly be part of the original structure. Undoubtedly the view is the chief reward for those who undertake the short but steep climb to the summit of the hill.

The Shahristan Bridge

The two most impressive of Isfahan's six bridges are Safavid work of the seventeenth century; but three or four miles down-stream there still stands a much older and more humble structure, the Pul-i-Shahristan, or Shahristan Bridge. Its great stone piers are probably Sasanian, and not a little indebted in their design to the Roman engineers who were taken prisoner along with their Emperor, Valerian; the upper part is of Seljuq brick, pierced by pointed arches which allow the maximum flow of water when the mountain snows melt. The bridge is sprawling, picturesque, decayed; and at its northern end there rise the remnants of two little pavilions.

The road from the town to the bridge follows the south bank of the river and is named the Dalan-i-Bihisht, or 'Passage to Paradise'. For a while it lives up to its name; but soon the shade-giving trees abruptly stop and the country becomes bleak and, in the summer months, almost unbearably dusty. After about an hour —if one has been rash enough to make the journey on foot—the bridge comes into

Fig. 3. Section through the small dome-chamber of the Friday Mosque (drawing by Eric Schroeder, from *A Survey of Persian Art*, by A. U. Pope).

sight and on the farther bank of the stream a small and crumbling village on rising ground. This hill was formerly crowned by a splendid Mongol minaret, the Minar--i-Shah Rustam, which was wantonly demolished in 1915; there still remain, however, a little *imamzadeh* (sanctuary of a saint) and the shell of a Safavid mosque.

Down by the stream there are willows, and in the spring if one sits by the water's edge in the bright sunshine, it is strange to reflect that this serene and silent spot was once the heart of Jay, the prosperous Sasanian city, and that even so late as the seventeenth century Chardin described Shahristan as one of the largest villages in the world.

The Portal of Jorjir

Near one of the gateways of the Hakim Mosque (*see* p. 149) is the beautiful incised-brick Portal of Jorjir, the only surviving monument of the tenth century. Long partially hidden by mud and brick walls, this unique structure was fully uncovered in 1955 by the Department of Antiquities. Of the rest of the Mosque, not a trace now remains.

The Friday Mosque (Masjid-i-Jami): Seljuq and Mongol work

If the Maidan and its surrounding buildings give the visitor the first flavour of the Isfahan of Shah Abbas, the Friday Mosque is the perfect introduction to what might perhaps be described as the 'pre-Abbas' city; for it is an epitome of Persian architecture from Seljuq to early Safavid times, and certainly also contains hidden vestiges of even earlier work.

The structures which remain from Seljuq and Mongol times include two Seljuq brick domechambers, the Mongol Sanctury of Öljaitu, and a vaulted labyrinth constructed at various periods between the twelfth and the fourteenth centuries. These buildings are notable for the sheer formal beauty of structural perfection.

A thirteenth-century Persian historian, Yaqut, stated that after Tughril Beg had captured Isfahan in 1051 the inhabitants were obliged, for lack of wood, to 'demolish' the Friday Mosque. Yet Nasir-i-Khusrau, who was there in 1052, found it 'great and magnificent'. Probably the explanation is that only the fittings, and perhaps some of the minor buildings, were actually destroyed; or it is possible that the destruction occurred after his visit. But almost immediately religious disturbances caused serious damage. Malik Shah, the Seljuq monarch, was a member of the Hanafite sect; Nizam al-Mulk, his powerful vizier and one of the greatest statesmen in Persian history, was a Shafi'ite. There is no need to look farther than Europe to learn of the bitterness of religious dispute; fighting broke out, during which the Shafi'ites destroyed 'a part of the southern building of the Mosque'. This undoubtedly included the dome and upper part of the walls of the larger dome-chamber, which constituted the Sanctury of the Mosque; these were at once rebuilt by the Nizam, as an inscription records. It bears no date; but the Nizam is known to have died in 1092.

Within a few years of the reconstruction of the Sanctuary, a smaller dome-chamber, sometimes known as the Gunbad-i-Khaki, or Brown Dome, was built on the northern boundary of the mosque. This is dated 1088-9 and was erected by Taj-ul-Mulk, counsellor of Shah Malik's mother and a sworn rival of the Nizam. If we are to see in it an attempt to surpass the Nizam's sanctuary, then Taj-ul-Mulk has certainly succeeded; though smaller, it is unquestionably the more perfect.

8. Detail of tile mosaic in the Friday Mosque.

The Gunbad-i-Khaki is austerity itself. 'The very material', wrote Robert By-

ron, ' is a signal of economy: hard small bricks of mousy grey, which swallow up the ornament of Kufic texts and stucco inlay in their puritan singleness of purpose'. The building is constructed in a succession of arches: first a single broad arch in the centre of each wall, with pairs of narrow arches cutting the corners; smaller arches in the squinches; and finally, sixteen little arches below the dome itself. The whole building is quite small: internally it is thirty-three feet square and sixty-five feet high. But it is doubtful whether there is another building in Persia, or in the whole of Islam, ' which offers so tense, so immediate an apparition of pure cubic form '.

The dome is a miracle of construction. The problem of setting a circular dome on a square base is one that has challenged generations of architects. Before New-

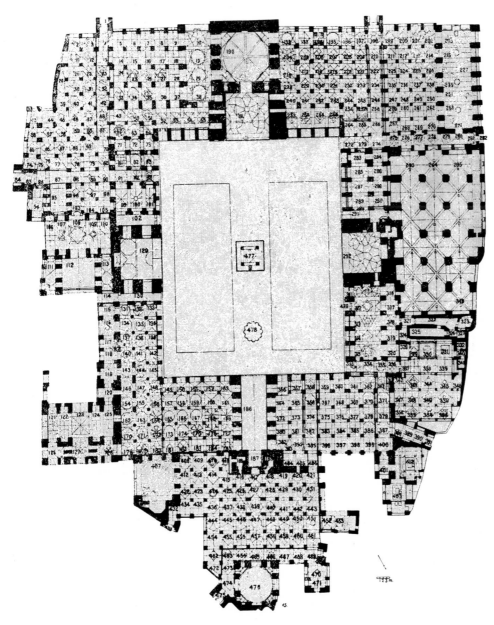

Fig. 4. Ground plan of the Friday Mosque (drawn by Eric Schroeder, from *A Survey of Persian Art*, by A. U. Pope).

9. Detail of brickwork from the complex of vaulted chambers in the Friday Mosque, dating from the twelfth to fourteenth centuries.

33

ton's work on the calculus, engineers in the West were unable to design a light dome of plain masonry; ten great chains grip the base of the dome of St Peter's, and even Wren, in St Paul's, made use of a concealed cone. But the Seljuqs

solved the difficulties which Wren *avoided*. Not that they knew anything of the calculus: their knowledge was empirical. But by courageous experiment and the intelligent observation of failure the Seljuqs built in the twelfth century what is practically the ideal dome, made possible by the advance of mathematical science in the eighteenth.[10]

To say that the Sanctuary falls short of the smaller dome-chamber in beauty of form, is to say no more than that it falls short of perfection. It is more stolid, more 'Norman' in character: 'twelve massive piers [wrote Byron] engage in a Promethean struggle with the weight of the dome'. If there is less homogeneity here than in the smaller chamber, the explanation may perhaps be found in the character of the lower part of the walls, which are probably a part of the original pre-Seljuq building. There is also the blue Safavid *mihrab* [11]—pretty enough in itself but discordant in this setting. This lack of complete unity is today emphasized by the rather abrupt transition from plaster below to brickwork above: the removal of this plaster world be an easy operation and would transform the appearance of the sanctuary.

On a simple gateway at the north-east side of the mosque is an inscription which records 'the reconstruction of this building after its burning, in the year 1121-2'. The exact extent of the damage is a matter of conjecture. Miraculously the two chambers survived, but probably most of the rest of the mosque was destroyed; at all events, no other visible parts of the extant building can be attributed to an earlier period. Recently, in the course of restoration which involved the temporary removal of tilework in order to repair the decayed masonry behind it, enough Seljuq brickwork was discovered to make it fairly certain that all the façades were rebuilt in plain brick under Sultan Sanjar (1118-57).

10. Detail of tile mosaic in the south-west *ivan* of the Friday Mosque, part of which is attributed to the fourteenth century.

Fig. 5. Main Court of the Friday Mosque (from *La Perse*, by Mme Dieulafoy, 1887).

Öljaitu Khudabandeh, who succeeded his brother Ghazan Khan, 'the Great Il-Khan',
in 1304, is best remembered for the vast but sadly ruined mosque which he built
at Sultaniyyeh to receive the bones of Ali and Husain; in the event it received
none but his own. The Great Il-Khan was a convert to Islam; Öljaitu (the name
means 'fortunate') wavered for a time between Islam and the old Mongol beliefs
until a dream, while he was visiting the tomb of Ali, finally convinced him of the
truth of the former.

The magnificent *mihrab* of Öljaitu in the Friday Mosque, dated 1310 and signed
as 'the work of Badr', is Öljaitu's memorial in Isfahan. The work is in chiselled
stucco—a craft with, even at that time, a millenium of history behind it; it shows
Naskhi calligraphy set against a complex foliate scrollwork, with borders of twisting
vine-leaves and a panel of what are usually described as lotus flowers. This *mihrab*
is the most elaborate but not the most subtle, example of Mongol stucco-work in
Iran. Splendid though it is, it is not integrated with the wall against which it is
set; it stands aloof, like a great altarpiece placed in a church for which it was not
designed. Moreover it has not the pleasant patina of age, but rather the grime of
stock brick in an industrial town.

PIR BAKRAN

In the neighbourhood of Isfahan, at Linjan and Astarjan, are further and more immediately attractive examples of Mongol stucco-work.[12]

About fifteen miles to the south-west of Isfahan is Linjan, a charming village situated in a little valley sheltered by gaunt mountains; it is a fitting setting for the
hermitage of Pir Bakran, a Sufi saint and mystic who taught and preached there
in the closing years of the thirteenth century. The site is clearly an ancient one,
its sanctity linked with a curious pot-hole in a rock which projects through the floor
of the sanctuary and which tradition alleges to be the footprint of Ali's horse. The
poet Firdausi is known to have taken refuge at Linjan after his flight from Ghazni
in the year 1011.

As Pir Bakran's renown spread, the original building—a little domed chamber—
proved too small for the crowds who flocked to attend his classes; his pupils therefore built a large *ivan* to afford them shelter. This stands upon a ledge of rock which,
while it adds to the impressiveness of the scale, made it necessary for entrance to
be through a meagre passage at the side. Worse still, a few years later, a wall
with a *mihrab* was added which completely blocks the open *ivan*. And, as so often
happens, the orientation of the *ivan* established an axis which did not correspond
with that of the sanctuary. The result is an agglomeration which is at once complex and incoherent, yet structurally of almost Sasanian simplicity. Much of the
material used is stone, not brick—another feature which links it with earlier methods
of construction.

The original mausoleum is a small, square and relatively dull building crowned
with a dome supported on four arches. What makes Pir Bakran a place of the
utmost interest to the artist and the archaeologist is the exquisite stucco ornament
of the *mihrabs* and over the doorways. These pieces of decoration must be studied
as individual objects, so haphazard is their apparent placing in the fabric as a whole.
They are closely related to the decoration of the *mihrab* of Öljaitu; but the work
here is almost more *art nouveau* in character, and in places bears a curious resem-
blance to decorative motives used in Nara, Japan, in the seventh century. Some
huge plaster panels of Kufic script are so highly stylized that they might almost serve
as designs for mazes.

11. Minaret of the Masjid-i-Ali
Seljuq work.

37

Pir Bakran died in 1303, before the work on the *ivan* had been completed, and an inscription dated 1312 records the enlargement which was carried out after his death. The saint's tomb is at the northern and covered end of the *ivan*, close to the wall of the original mausoleum.[13]

ASTARJAN

The Friday Mosque at Astarjan, about twenty-five miles to the west of Isfahan, may—and undoubtedly should—be included in any expedition to Pir Bakran. The peculiar feature of this building, which is one of the loveliest of all fourteenth-century mosques in Iran, is the narrowness of all its component parts; this narrowness, as dramatic as it is unexpected, serves to emphasize its height.

The entrance portal, which is surmounted by twin cylindrical minarets, leads to a curiously long and narrow court surrounded by prayer halls, one of which is below ground level. The lofty sanctuary, with its beautifully fretted polychrome dome, contains the highest *mihrab* in all Iran; it is also unusual in being integrated with the structure and not simply an object applied to a wall already standing. The stucco work, with stalactites and rope moulding, is very striking. One of the smaller *mihrabs* has been moved to the Archaeological Museum in Tehran. In a portal at the back of the mosque are some of the brightest gentian-blue tiles in all Iran.

MINARETS

The *minar*, or minaret, was designed to serve the same purpose in Islam that the belfry serves in Christendom: the summons to worship. There was always the danger that, from the summit of a minaret, the *muezzin* might be able to observe too much of what went on in the women's quarters, and blind *muezzins* were employed for the Royal Mosque, whose minarets commanded a view of the royal harem. Today in Iran the *muezzin* is more often to be heard from a small pent-house situated above one of the *ivans* or even, more audibly but less romantically, through a loud-speaker.

It seems that the origin of the minaret must be sought in Syria in the time of the Umayyads. The form generally adopted in Iran was a slightly tapering cylindrical shaft. Records exist of forty-three minarets in and around Isfahan, thirty-two of which were in the city itself, and doubtless the list is far from complete. In fact, Isfahan must once have been dominated by minarets in the way that Bologna, Siena and San Gimignano were dominated by towers.

A handful of minarets dating from Seljuq and Mongol times still survives in various parts of the city, and of others there remain the bases or a much-mutilated shaft. Tall, ruinous, stripped of most of their trimmings, they do in fact from a distance suggest industry rather than religion; but closer inspection shows the beauty of their intricate brickwork and the occasional survival of a brick or tiled inscription.

The earliest is probably the minaret of the Masjid-i-Ali, built around the close of the eleventh century and now attached to a Safavid mosque. There still remains nearly 160 feet of relatively well preserved brick column, and the crumbled summit has recently been restored. It rises not far from the Friday Mosque, and is the most conspicuous and easily accessible of these early minarets in Isfahan.

The Chihil Dukhtaran ('Forty Daughters') minaret is also Seljuq, with a Kufic inscription on the base bearing the date 1107-8; with one exception it is the earliest dated minaret in Iran, and contains a novel feature in the large window pierced about two-thirds of the way up the shaft. From the latter part of the

12. The Mausoleum of Baba Qasim. The handsome tree-shaded portal is dated A. D. 1340.

38

13

14

twelfth century are the Masjid-i-Shaya and Sarban minarets; all these three are to be found in Yahudiyyeh, to the north-east of the Maidan. The Sarban minaret, also known as the 'minaret of the camel-drivers', is the finest of all those that survive in the city itself; one hundred and fifty feet in height, it has two delicate but rather damaged girdles of stalactite ornament, and bands of Kufic inscriptions in brick and blue tilework.

Two pairs of Mongol minarets are of special interest, the more impressive being the Do Minar Dar al-Diafeh in Yahudiyyeh. The twin columns rise on each side

Fig. 6. Signal Tower at Isfahan (from *La Perse*, by Mme Dieulafoy, 1887).

13. Distant view of the Friday Mosque showing the dome of the Sanctuary and the *ivan* through which it is approached.

14. Tile mosaic from the Friday Mosque.

15. The Darb-i-Imam, A.D. 1453.
This is one
of the many peaceful courts
to be found in the less-frequented
mosques.

16. Detail of tile mosaic from
the *ivan* of the Darb-i-Imam.

Fig. 7. Mongol brick minaret at Isfahan (now destroyed), (from *La Perse*, by Mme Dieulafoy, 1887).

42

of a modern arch, the Dar al-Battikh, which spans the street; the effect is somewhat like that of the entrance to a mosque whose *ivan* is disproportionately small. The other pair of minarets, the Do Minar Dardasht, is to be found beside the ruined tomb-chamber of a lady named Bakht-i-Aqa, not far from the Friday Mosque; it shows the typical Mongol use of second-hand brick, mud brick, and faience in spiral bands. The tops of the minarets have fallen, and on the summit of one of the broken columns a stork has now built her nest.

Of the Masjid-i-Qushkhaneh ('Falcon Mosque'), which stood in open country on the northern outskirts of Isfahan, nothing remains but the minaret, whose delicate tiling suggests early Timurid work of about 1400. Probably Timurid also was the handsome Khwajeh Alam minaret which Pope was able to photograph [14] shortly before its regrettable demolition in 1934.

The Shaking Minarets

These are the principal pre-Safavid minarets but no visitor to Isfahan can escape being conducted to the much over-rated Minar-i-Jumban, or 'Shaking Minarets'. They stand guard over a pretty little Mongol mosque, about three miles to the west of the town, with an *ivan* dated 1317 which fully justifies the expedition. Beneath the *ivan*, in a large rectangular chest, lies the body of a sufi Shaikh, who died in 1338.

The famous minarets—small brick towers rising some twenty feet above the *ivan*— probably date from the eighteenth century, and must inevitably be mentioned in any book on Isfahan. Spiral staircases lead to their summits, which are pierced with open arches. When the custodian ascends one of the minarets and, swaying to and fro, vigorously pushes against the wall, the minaret oscillates. What is curious is that this movement is transmitted to the other minaret also.

Dr Wills, who was in Isfahan about eighty years ago, describes the whole thing as 'a terrible fraud'. Fraud it is not: it is merely, as Lord Curzon says, 'a commonplace, even if uncommon, manifestation'—a mild conjuring-trick to amuse simple minds. But the pious naturally sought a supernatural explanation: the movement, they said, was caused by the sufi saint, who was still alive in his tomb. Rationalists succeeded, somehow or other, in getting the tomb opened, so establishing beyond any doubt that the saint was dead.

> The situation grew serious, and European savants became involved. They declared that the minarets were erected on the ends of a horizontal beam balanced on the extrados of the arch. But the explanation is hardly plausible, for in that case there would be an up-and-down movement as well as oscillation. Moreover no piece of timber would be strong enough to support a weight such as that of the minarets without breaking.[15]

Various suggestions have been made to account rationally for the 'miracle'. Mme Dieulafoy believed that each of the minarets was supported by a central verticle beam, fixed in a kind of socket. The minarets, she says, can make small oscillations round this vertical axis, though this movement is visible only at the top; reverberations thus set up spread, by way of the tympanum, from one minaret to the other. Curzon doubts this: 'More probably', he says, 'the elasticity of the bricks and mortar employed have something to do with it, the vibration easily excited in one tower then being communicated along the tympanum of the main arch to the other'.[16]

Imamzadeh Ja'far

Not far from the junction of the Khiaban-i-Hafiz and the Khiaban-i-Hatif stands the Mongol Imamzadeh Ja'far, a small octagonal shrine erected in 1325, externally

17. The Lutfullah Mosque, A. D. 1603, seen from the terrace of the Ali Qapu.

45

of pale-coloured brick but with spandrels filled with tile-mosaic. Very probably it was once surmounted by a conical roof of the kind often found on shrines of this period in various parts of Iran. This is one of the innumerable ' tombs ' of Ja'far, the companion of Muhammad, none of which in fact contains his bones. It is an elegant, well-proportioned building, and highly venerated by Moslems. Unfortunately it suffered rather excessive restoration in 1950.

The Mausoleum of Baba Qasim

Of almost exactly the same date, but of greater charm, is the Mausoleum of Baba Qasim, situated to the north of the Friday Mosque. A few steps lead down to the pretty, tree-shaded stalactite portal, with fine tile-work bearing the date 1340. Beyond is the tomb-chamber, with a damaged but very handsome *mihrab*, and a ' ribbed ' dome of a kind that was to become very fashionable in the following century.

Fig. 8. The Imamzadeh Ja'far before restoration (from *La Perse*, by Mme Dieulafoy, 1887).

Baba Qasim was a Persian theologian—a Sunni, as is shown by inscriptions giving the names of the Caliphs Abu Bekr, Omar and Othman. Sir John Chardin wrote that witnesses who testified falsely on the tomb 'suddenly burst, and their bowels gushed out'; for a time, therefore, it was much in demand by honest litigants. But the mausoleum fell on evil days: the tomb disappeared, to be replaced (for some reason or other) by that of a bath-towel manufacturer who worked no miracles. By 1928, the building was being used to stable a donkey belonging to a neighbouring grocer; but it has now been tidied up and restored. The external tent-dome is relatively modern, probably dating from the nineteenth century.

Adjoining the tomb of Baba Qasim, and closely associated with it, is the Madraseh Imami—a pretty building with a four-*ivan* court and good brickwork. The tile-work both here and in the Mausoleum shows the earliest phase of the transformation from purely geometrical design to the intricate floral patterns that reached perfection under the Timurids in the fifteenth century. This is one of the 'national monuments' that has not yet been taken in hand by the Department of Antiquities. The brick work is cracking, the tiles are falling; the picturesque but squalid court is full of hens and washing and children. Old photographs show that, even as recently as thirty years ago, most of the finest buildings in Isfahan were in a similar state of neglect.

THE TIMURIDS

Tamerlane, it has already been mentioned, captured Isfahan in 1386, massacring its inhabitants but sparing its buildings. The vital centres for the development of Islamic architecture were now transferred from western Iran, first to his new capital, Samarqand (Russian Turkestan), and then, under his son Shah Rukh, to Herat (Afghanistan) and Meshed (eastern Iran). There appears to have been no further building in Isfahan until almost the middle of the fifteenth century; indeed, craftsmen, particularly tile-makers, are known to have left Isfahan and other western towns to work for Tamerlane at Samarqand.

For the visitor to Isfahan this is a misfortune, for the Timurid renaissance produced, in the late fourteenth and early fifteenth centuries, some of the finest of all Islamic buildings: the Gur-i-Mir (tomb of Tamerlane) at Samarqand; the great palace at Kesh, now so ruined that its magnificence can only be estimated from Clavijo's account of his embassy to Tamerlane; the Gauhar Shad Mosque at Meshed, and the group of buildings associated with the Shah's wife, but now sadly ruined, at Herat; the nearby Gozar Gah which was rebuilt by her husband, Shah Rukh; and the famous Blue Mosque at Tabriz. However, the high renaissance of Timurid building (1450-1500), in which decoration was still more splendid and hardly less pure, is represented, in quality if not in great quantity, in Isfahan. There are also examples of early Safavid work in which eastern artisans clearly played a large part.

What did the Timurids contribute to the development of Islamic architecture? To estimate their achievement it is necessary, as Robert Byron points out, to distinguish between what they inherited and what they invented. 'The history of Muhammadan architecture in Persia suggests at times', he wrote, 'the action of a structural impulse, arriving from the north-east in the wake of Turkish invaders, on the Persian habit of surface decoration. The Timurids, like the Seljuqs and Mongols before them, revived this impulse'.[17] This is his personal, and it would seem very plausible, explanation; other authorities consider that the 'structural impulse' was native to Iran and never wholly submerged.

The chief structural contribution of the Timurids was their development of the pendentive, until finally it assumed the elaborate 'stalactite' form which the West finds so characteristic of Islamic architecture. But far more important was their extension of the possibilities of the faience tile. The use of tiles in Islamic architecture was, of course, nothing new. Already as early as the eleventh century, lustre tiles were being manufactured in some quantity; but the superior advantages of faience mosaic, composed of a jigsaw of cut monochrome tiles, soon became apparent. It was cheaper, more durable, and far better suited to the decoration of large areas.

The first self-colour to be used was turquoise. To this were soon added mirror black, white, and lapis lazuli. In the fourteenth century came a rich buttercup yellow which was developed to give shades ranging from pale buff to deep saffron. Finally came emerald green, and an aubergine that fluctuated through garnet to a tone that was almost black. In the fifteenth century use was also sometimes made, in very small quantities, of a bright red unglazed clay.

The Timurid builders inherited the tradition of tile-work employed merely as an ornament quite subsidiary to structure; they left behind them buildings that glowed and glittered with colour, but whose structural qualities were not swamped or obscured by it.

> At a first glance the chief characteristic of the new style is ostentation. Domes and minarets protrude and multiply; portals, *ivans*, and niche-façades attain extraordinary height; patterns and texts become exuberant in proportion to their intricacy ... unbridled, fantastic; colour achieves a range, a depth, and a brilliance not equalled before or since ... Aesthetically, the achievement of the new style was to devise a method of displaying colour without prejudice to an appearance of stability and coherence. This it did by the propriety of its general proportions and detailed ratios, by splitting the ornament into fields related to those elements, and by a subtle play of reveals, bevels, and kindred means of emphasis and punctuation—by using, in fact, a language common to all good architecture. Timurid buildings sit the ground, and prove that their architects, though providing a show in two dimensions, were still able to think in three.[18]

In 1447 a hall for winter prayers was added to the Friday Mosque in Isfahan. The building of it is recorded in a magnificent faience recess close to the *mihrab* of Öljaitu, the artist's name being given as Sayyid Mahmud. Further Timurid work in this Mosque is to be found within the south-west *ivan*, which was restored and redecorated under Uzun Hasan in 1475-6. The scale of its tile-panels is tremendous, the designs magnificent, the technique unusual: 'individual elements—stars large and small, and various polygons including half octagons—were rendered separately in faience mosaic and attached to the background which is in the same technique, standing out in marked relief'.[19]

This type of decoration occurs nowhere in western Iran outside Isfahan, though it was used in Transoxiana and at a later date in Meshed. Another splendid example of it is to be seen in the Darb-i-Imam, near the Friday Mosque in Isfahan. Here two domes rise above the tombs of two sons of *imams*; but the tile-work in question, which hardly has its equal, is to be found in the portal. In front of this portal there stands a stone lion devouring a man of whom the moustached head alone remains visible; women believe that the act of passing three times under the belly of the lion is a cure for sterility. A most remarkable stained glass window, formerly in one of the tomb chambers, has been transferred to the audience hall of the Chihil Sutun.

18. Tile mosaic decorating the dome of the Lutfullah Mosque, A.D. 1603.

The first Safavids

As THE FIFTEENTH CENTURY drew to its close, Persia awaited the advent of a ruler strong enough to reunite the kingdom and hold it together. Such a man appeared in a certain Ismail, who in 1499, after a succession of smaller victories in north-west Persia, seized Tabriz and was proclaimed first Shah of the Safavid dynasty. This was the first truly Persian dynasty for many centuries, and one which was to rule for more than 200 years. Of this line, Shah Abbas the Great was the fifth ruler; and although his four predecessors were only indirectly concerned with Isfahan, it is of importance to sketch, very briefly, their careers and achievements.

Ismail was descended from the fifth *Imam*, his family renowned for piety no less than for bravery. His mother, Martha, was the daughter of Uzun Hasan by a Greek princess. As a Shi'ite, Ismail was particularly acceptable to the Persians, who had always viewed Sunni doctrines with suspicion.

The chief problem that confronted Ismail, and his successors for more than a century after, was the perpetual threat of invasion by the Ottoman Turks from the West and the Özbegs from the East. This war on two fronts continued with changing fortune: Baghdad, Mosul and Diarbekr fell to Ismail, who then remained on the defensive in the West while he drove the Özbegs from Balkh and Herat. But the Ottoman Selim the Grim seized Tabriz and began to advance farther into Persia. Persian troops were rushed westwards: Tabriz was recovered, but the Özbegs regained Transoxiana.

Ismail died in 1524, leaving his son, Tahmasp, to continue a struggle with constantly-changing fortune. During his lifetime Ismail was worshipped by his subjects as a saint; so great was their faith in him that they often went unarmed into battle. An Italian merchant, Angiolello, who saw him frequently, tells us that he was good-looking and attractive, red-headed, left-handed, and 'brave as a gamecock'.[20]

Tahmasp, a boy of ten when Ismail died, inherited a redoubtable Ottoman opponent in Sulaiman the Magnificent, who for a time held Tabriz and Isfahan; he made Qazvin his capital. He is remembered for the unusual length of his reign (fifty-two years); his treachery in selling his guest Bayazid, Sulaiman's son, to his father in exchange for 400,000 pieces of gold; and for a mention (as 'Bactrian Sophi') in *Paradise Lost*. The claim sometimes made, that he was the Louis XIV of Persia, is hard to substantiate.

In Tahmasp's reign Anthony Jenkinson, a typical English merchant-adventurer of the period, reached Persia by way of Russia with letters from Queen Elizabeth. Repulsed at first by the Shah as an 'unbeliever', he hurriedly left the palace 'followed by a man with a basanet of sand, sifting all the way that I had gone'; but subsequently he was more cordially received. In the end, however, it was found impossible for him to trade by such devious routes.

Some kind of a peace with the Ottoman Turks was established in 1555, and the later years of Tahmasp's reign were relatively uneventful. D'Alessandri,[21] sent as an ambassador by the Venetians in 1571, formed a poor opinion of the Shah, who cared only for money and women and who had not set foot outside his palace for

19. Portal of the Lutfullah Mosque, a splendid example of stalactite decoration.

eleven years. He found the roads unsafe, the judges venal, and the country neglected.

In 1576 Tahmasp was poisoned by one of his women, and after endless intrigues and not a few assassinations his fourth son succeeded him as Ismail II. Ismail had been held in prison by his father for twenty-five years; brutalized by his long captivity, he began his reign by putting to death most of his more dangerous rivals. For a time his eldest brother, Muhammad Khudabandeh, purblind and seemingly innocuous as Governor of Khorasan, was left in peace; finally, however, Ismail gave orders for him and his young son, Abbas, to be assassinated. But before this order could be carried out, Ismail suddenly died—some say of drink and an overdose of opium, others that he was murdered by fifteen men disguised as women—and Muhammad Khudabandeh ascended the throne he was quite unfit to occupy.

Civil war broke out; the Turks seized the opportunity to invade and again took Tabriz. In 1587 Khorasan proclaimed Abbas Shah, and his unlamented father vanished from the scene.

EARLY SAFAVID ARCHITECTURE

It was the 'minor' arts of carpet-weaving, textiles, miniature-painting and pottery which flourished most vigorously under the early Safavids (*see* p. 118). Fate has been unkind to their buildings: of Ismail's great palace at Khoy, between Tabriz and the Turkish frontier, not a trace remains; but some idea of its splendour can be gathered from the writings of an anonymous Italian merchant who was in Persia between 1507 and 1520.[22] Vanished also is the 'Sengerie' Mosque in Isfahan, which bore Shah Ismail's name in letters of gold. But in Isfahan there can still be seen two buildings which date for the most part from his reign.

The portal of the first of these, the rambling and frequently renovated Mausoleum of Harun Vilayet, gives more than a taste of the magical quality of early Safavid tile-work. The interlocking arabesques in the spandrels of the outer portal arches are delicate as the borders of an illuminated manuscript; the panels that flank the inner doorway are as rich in colour and as intricate in design as the best Persian rugs. An inscription in faience records that this tile-mosaic was the work of one Husain and made in the reign of ' the victorious Shah Ismail Bahadur Khan, may the portals of the blessings of Paradise be opened to him, 1512 ', and Chardin adds the information that the Grand Vizier Durmish Khan paid for it. An insignificant doorway to the left leads to the shrine, which is much frequented by women in the belief that it offers a cure for sterility. The Christian is unwelcome.

Close to this Mausoleum stands the Mosque of Ali, whose Seljuq minaret has already been mentioned. Here again is magnificent tile-work and splendid calligraphy. For the latter a Tabrizi, Shams ud-Din, was responsible; ' Musaddiq the tile-cutter ' probably designed the whole façade, for his signature, together with a chronogram giving the year 1522, appears in the place of honour above the principal entrance. From the roof there is a fine view of the city.

There is probably no important extant monument which can be assigned to Shah Tahmasp or to his long and successful reign. The palace and mosque that he built at Qazvin, his capital, were destroyed by an earthquake early in the nineteenth century; his mosque at Tabriz, his caravanserai near Sultaniyeh, his summer residences at Kharagan and Surley, are all no more. This was in part due to the taste of the monarch, who himself painted and designed carpets but showed less interest in architecture. For the rest, the reckless use at this time of unfired bricks was to result in the fall of Safavid domes while neighbouring Seljuq domes survived.

But not all was wholly destroyed. In Isfahan the portal of the Qutbiyeh Mosque, which has now been re-erected in the gardens of the Chihil Sutun, carries an inscription to the effect that it was dedicated in honour of Tahmasp and that the artist was 'Qasim of Tabriz'. The finest extant tile mosaics of his reign are, however, those in the revetments of the south-west *ivan* of the Friday Mosque in Isfahan. 'The technique is admirable, the colours brilliant, the patterns splendid', wrote Pope. 'Framing the portal arch is a magnificent *tabula ansata* chain with very handsome calligraphy, exactly like the borders of the Tabriz carpets of the day'.[23]

Fig. 9.   Pierced Steel Plate, *Victoria and Albert Museum*.

Part 2   Shah Abbas the Great (1587-1629)

UNTIL THE closing years of the sixteenth century, those Europeans who visited Isfahan had carried back but little information about what was, after all, no more than a provincial capital. When, in 1598, Shah Abbas decided to promote Isfahan to the metropolis of his kingdom, to embellish it, and to encourage trade and intercourse with the West, a concourse of cultured foreigners flocked to his court and to those of his successors. Many published accounts (*see* Bibliography) of their travels, and from these it is possible to form a very exact picture of Isfahan at the height of its splendour. Some of the most interesting of these books, and their authors, may be mentioned here.

The astonishing adventures of the two Sherley (or Shirley) brothers, Sir Anthony and Sir Robert, have been fully described elsewhere and are only briefly touched upon here. In 1598 Anthony, then a man in his early thirties with a dozen or more years of buccaneering and adventure already behind him, left Venice for Persia with his younger brother Robert, a youth of about seventeen. The objects of his journey were to urge Abbas to ally himself with the Christian princes against the Ottoman Turk, and to reopen trade relations with England; he alleged that he travelled under the auspices of Essex, but the English government disowned him.

At Qazvin the two brothers were received by Abbas, who sent Anthony as his ambassador to various courts of Europe. Robert remained in Persia, where he helped to reorganize the Persian army; he married a Circassian, who in 1607 accompanied him to Europe as the Shah's ambassador. In 1615 he was in Isfahan, when Abbas again despatched him to Europe. In London he quarrelled furiously with a Persian envoy of the Shah, a man named Najdi Beg, and in 1627 the two men were sent back to Persia in separate ships, Robert being accompanied by an English ambassador, Sir Dodmore Cotton, and Sir Thomas Herbert. Robert, the victim of conspiracies at the Persian court, was coolly received by Abbas; bitterly disappointed that his work had not been appreciated, he fell ill and died a few weeks later. The Shah was afterwards filled with remorse, declaring (wrote Herbert) that Robert ' had done more for him than any of his native subjects '.

From Italy in 1617 came the wealthy Roman patrician Pietro Della Valle, with the Nestorian wife he had married in Baghdad. They remained for nearly five years in Persia, a good part of that time being spent in Isfahan. Della Valle saw Abbas frequently, and gives a detailed and faithful account of the capital in a series of letters addressed to his friend Schipano in Naples.

Abbas's tolerance (as a rule) of Christianity resulted in the establishment of various Roman Catholic missions in Isfahan and Julfa—first of the Augustinians (1603), then of the Carmelites (1608) and later of the Capuchins. The Augustinian Antonio di Govea, and several of the Carmelites, have left valuable reports which throw much light on the complex character of Abbas, whom they came to know well. Père Sanson, a secular chaplain, wrote of Isfahan under Shah Sulaiman at the end of the seventeenth century.

20. Imamzadeh Ja'far, Mongol work, A. D. 1325. This building has suffered from excessive restoration.

54

Sir Thomas Herbert, the twenty-year-old youth who accompanied Robert Sherley and Cotton to Persia in 1627, spent three weeks in Isfahan the following spring. His book, *A Relation of some Years Travaile*, is by far the most entertaining of the early Persian travelogues. Four editions were called for, each enlarged (to little advantage) by the inclusion of second-hand material till the final edition had become almost four times the length of the first.

Jean-Baptiste Tavernier, a famous French jeweller, was more than once in Isfahan —for the first time in 1632 when Abbas's successor, Shah Safi, was on the throne, and for the last time in 1664 during the reign of Shah Abbas II. On the latter journey he was accompanied by André Daulier-Déslandes, who also left an account of his travels. Tavernier's *Six Voyages* has been much criticized. It was said that he knew no Persian, and even that he could neither read nor write, but the picture that he draws of Isfahan is of especial interest in that it appears to be the only seventeenth-century study of the city which is wholly free of exaggerated praise; indeed Tavernier thought very poorly of many of the buildings, streets and gardens which so excited most of his contemporaries. Tavernier died in Moscow in 1689 when on his way once again to Persia, at the age of eighty-four.[24]

These are some of the men—English, French, German, Dutch, Spanish and Italian—who came to the courts of the Safavid Shahs as ambassadors, missionaries, merchants, adventurers, scholars or dilettantes, and who by their writings revealed to their eager countrymen the splendours of the capital that Abbas had created. The large majority of these travellers behaved well and so deserved the good treatment that they were in general accorded by the Safavid Shahs and especially by Abbas the Great, but the same could not be said of the Portuguese Augustinian Fathers resident in Hormuz, whose excessive zeal led them to use force in the conversion of reluctant Muslim children. Father Paul Simon, a Carmelite in Isfahan in the reign of Abbas the Great, wrote:

> The good treatment and favouritism afforded the Franks [i.e. Europeans] by the King of Persia is the more marked because, notwithstanding what the Christian princes have said to him, and notwithstanding the injuries inflicted on his people in Hormuz, he has never allowed the slightest injustice to be done to our merchants on their way overland to India, nor has he lost the respect he used to pay to Franks who came to this country, where some of them, and Italians too, have caused no small scandal, and committed many follies, such as to get drunk and when drunk to dash about the Maidan at a gallop, striking this and that Persian, and killing one or other of them, of which the city of Isfahan made complaint to the King—all the same the King did not wish them to be condemned to death because they were Franks, although he is very severe with his own people, even when they be governors and nobles of the realm....[25]

SHAH ABBAS

Abel Pinçon, a Frenchman in the suite of Sir Anthony Sherley, has described Abbas as he appeared in 1599. The Shah was then about twenty-eight, short and well-built, good-looking, with black hair and beard and a complexion no darker than a Spaniard's. He was quick in mind and agile in body, very affable to strangers, and especially to Christians.

The beard was soon discarded in favour of big mustachios which drooped a little because it was presumptuous to train them heavenwards. In portraits of him these appear slightly comical to Western eyes, but in actual life they gave him a certain *panache*; even at his most informal—and Abbas enormously enjoyed ' unbending '— he was always dignified and impressive.

One of the Carmelites, Father John Thaddeus, gives a brilliant sketch of his appearance in 1624, when Abbas was about fifty-three, and of his character.[26] By this time the Shah had grown rather plump, and some of his front teeth were missing. His head was completely shaved, his mustachios grey, his face tanned almost black

21. The Ali Qapu Palace, serving as a gateway to the Palace grounds (early seventeenth century).

57

by the sun ('though they say that the skin of his body is white'). Herbert, four years later gives the additional information that his eyes were 'small and flaming', and that they had no eye-lashes. Father John considered Abbas 'bright-witted, martial, mercurial, strong, skilful, healthy, resolute, with a good memory, and sagacious in business'; his facial expression changed with his mood from 'jolly' to 'that of a raging lion'.

Very energetic by nature, Abbas particularly disliked laziness in others. He loved hunting, and often busied himself in the royal stables. He was a skilled craftsman,

Fig. 10. Shah Abbas the Great (from *A Description of the Persian Monarchy*, by Sir Thomas Herbert, 1634).

making scimitars, arquebuses, bridles and saddles for his horses, weaving cloth and distilling orange-flower water with his own hands. Sometimes he gutted the fish or skinned and cut up the game he had killed, and cooked it himself. Very skilful with a knife, he could geld a slave as deftly as any surgeon in his kingdom.

In a discussion, Abbas was quick at getting the point: the merest hint of a matter was enough. He loved a good argument; though almost illiterate, he was a skilful dialectician, knowing all the tricks of the trade and always ready to cap an opponent's remark with a sharp and well-aimed thrust. He listened to what others had to say, then replied briskly and pointedly. He was eager to learn about foreign lands, and never missed an opportunity of cross-examining visitors from Europe about conditions in their home countries.

Extremely superstitious, he always took the advice of his astrologers. Della Valle mentions that on one occasion Abbas camped outside the walls of Isfahan until a day was proclaimed as auspicious for his entry into the city. This blind faith in the stars was responsible for the curious episode of his temporary abdication in 1591. Having been told by the court astrologer that the configuration of the planets threatened the occupant of the throne, he made a certain Yusuf, who was probably a Christian, Shah until the danger was over. Yusuf was crowned and enjoyed four days of glory; on the fifth day he was executed.

Cautious for his life, Abbas perpetually changed his bedroom to defeat attempts at assassination; yet he was not afraid to ride through the city with no other protection than that of a single servant. He generally dressed simply, though on formal occasions he wore rich brocades and jewels and looked every inch a king. On festival days he usually wore red silk with a scarlet tunic, but when he was with his army he went poorly clad and in rope shoes.

Like many oriental monarchs he enjoyed going about among his subjects, and not infrequently he went incognito. He would sit down anywhere and give audiences—' even just in his shirt and drawers '—and he cared little what or where he ate. Sometimes he would ride out to Julfa, the Armenian colony that he had founded in the southern suburbs of Isfahan, and enter

> the house of a private person and sit there two or three hours drinking with him and finding out what he wants to know ... He is also wont to go for a pastime to other places hardly respectable, such as to his kitchen, which is a house separate from the palace, and sit down there, eating whatever pleased him. Sometimes passing through the city on foot he will come to the shops of the greengrocers, fruiterers, and those who sell preserves and sweetmeats. Here he will take a mouthful of this, there another of that—in one place sample a preserve, in another taste some fruit. Or he will enter the shop of a shoemaker, pick up a pair of shoes that takes his fancy, put them on at the door and then continue on his way. On one occasion when he was wandering about like this he said to some of the Augustinian Fathers, ' How do you feel about what I am doing, Fathers? I am a king after my own will, and to go about in this way is to be a king— not like yours, who is always sitting indoors! ' [27]

Naturally Abbas was curious about Christianity, as he was about everything from the West, and showed a good deal of tolerance towards Christians; but that he ever seriously played with the idea of himself becoming a Christian (as is sometimes alleged) is highly improbable, though it amused him to encourage this hope in the missionaries.

As to Abbas's vices, there is little doubt that, like most oriental monarchs, he was a sodomite. Besides his wives and his harem of several hundred women, he kept ' more than two hundred boys '. When he went to any place ' he would cause the best-looking boys to be lined up at the entrance ', and ' thirty or forty naked boys ' used to accompany him to the baths. Father John Thaddeus alleges that Abbas introduced sodomy into Persia, ' where hitherto it had been abhorred '; but this cannot be believed.

More serious was his cruelty, excessive even by oriental standards of the day; it equalled that of his infamous contemporary, Ivan the Terrible of Russia.

> He succeeded his father by having his brothers suppressed; he killed or mutilated his own three sons. For a mere suspicion, a fit of temper, or a jest, he killed nobles and subjects. A single shadow across his ambition was a capital crime in itself, and he was wont to say that he would have killed a hundred children in order to reign alone for a single day.[28]

THE NEW CAPITAL

On his accession to the throne, Abbas inherited the danger that had overshadowed the reigns of his Safavid predecessors—the perpetual threat of invasion on two fronts.

On the eastern borders of his kingdom the predatory Özbegs were in their usual state of revolt; in the north-west, the Ottoman Turks still held Persian territory which they had overrun earlier in the century. Abbas was not strong enough to make war against Turk and Özbeg simultaneously, but by good fortune the Turks, at that moment, were fully occupied on the Hungarian borders and in no position to take the offensive against the Persians. Abbas therefore seized the opportunity to attack the Özbegs, whom he finally reduced to submission in the summer of 1598. For much of the rest of his reign, especially during the closing years, he was inter-mittently at war with the Turks, and in the main victorious. At the time of his death his dominions stretched from the Tigris almost to the Indus.

It was in the spring of 1598 that Abbas transferred his capital from Qazvin to Isfahan. Both Qazvin and the earlier Safavid capital, Tabriz, were dangerously exposed to Turkish attack; indeed, Tabriz had more than once fallen to the enemy. Isfahan, on the other hand, was fairly centrally placed; it had an excellent climate, and great reserves of water not far below the ground. Furthermore, it was the capi-tal of the province and ancient kingdom of Fars, from which the word 'Persia' is derived. There was probably an additional and more personal reason for Abbas's decision: he liked Isfahan, and had often stayed there in the little Timurid palace built by Shah Tahmasp in the large park called the Naqsh-i-Jihan, or 'Picture of the World'.

With the Özbegs subdued and the Turks still fully occupied elsewhere, there en-sued a lustrum of relative peace which gave Abbas the opportunity to begin the adornment of his new capital. He found Isfahan a large provincial town not wholly lacking in good buildings; he left it the equal of Cairo or Constantinople—that is to say, one of the greatest cities in the world. In 1598 its very name was little known outside western Asia; thirty years later, its fame had spread to all the courts of Europe.

As in the far distant days of Darius, artists and craftsmen were summoned from remote countries—from Italy, from India, and later even from China—to supplement local talent. Not that talent was lacking in Persia: Persian architects, in particu-lar, designed nobly. That under Abbas's direction they often built badly, was their misfortune rather than their fault. Royal impatience commanded swift results and would not take 'No' for an answer. There is a well-known story, probably apocry-phal, concerning the building of the Royal Mosque. Abbas ordered work on the walls to be begun; the architect refused, saying that the foundations had not yet set. Abbas grew angry; the architect therefore took careful measurements and, very sensibly, went into hiding. When he judged that the time was ripe to prove his point, he reappeared, demonstrated the accuracy of his forecast, and was ac-corded the royal pardon. Nevertheless there is no doubt that a great deal of shoddy building was in fact carried out in parts of the Royal Mosque, as those who have recently had the task of restoring it know to their cost.

There was already a Maidan in the city (the Maidan-i-Kuhneh, or 'Old Square') when Abbas adopted it as his capital; probably it covered an area to the south-west of the Friday Mosque. It is said that Abbas at first considered retaining and enlarging it; when, however, a truculent landowner made difficulties over the sale of his property, Abbas decided to ruin him by moving the centre of the city's life elsewhere. His thoughts turned, very naturally, to the Naqsh-i-Jihan. The little Palace was heightened by several storeys and enlarged into the present Ali Qapu, and the new Maidan designed so that the palace commanded a view of it. In the Naqsh-i-Jihan he built further palaces for himself and for his women.

Abbas's buildings fall fairly exactly into two groups. In the first period, roughly from 1598 to 1606, the Maidan, the Ali Qapu, the Chahar Bagh avenue, together with the Allahverdi Khan Bridge across the river, the Lutfullah, Maqsud Beg and

22. Niches in one o the music rooms at the top of the Ali Qapu.

Surkhi Mosques were laid out. Then troubles with the Turks put a halt to building, which was not resumed until about 1612. The second part of the programme was principally concerned with the completion of the buildings round the Maidan—in particular the Royal Mosque, which was not in fact quite finished at the time of Abbas's death, and the entrance to the Royal Bazaar. Within the Palace may also now have been erected the building which was reconstructed under Abbas II and is known as the Chihil Sutun.[29]

THE MAIDAN

' Let me lead you ', wrote Herbert, ' into the Maidan ... without doubt as spacious, as pleasant and aromatic a market as any in the universe '. We will allow him to do so, and, seated upon one of the new municipal benches,[30] try to reconstruct the scene as it would have appeared in its heyday in the seventeenth century.

The backcloth is still today much as it was then—the long arcaded walls magnificently broken by the four principal buildings that dominate the square: the Royal Mosque, the Shaikh Lutfullah Mosque, the Ali Qapu and the portal of the Qaisariyeh, or Royal Bazaar. In the central part of the Maidan there was no permanent structure except a tall mast or maypole;[31] but at each end of the square was the pair of marble polo goalposts, which still survive. Round the perimeter of the square, water flowed in a stone-edged canal which was lined with a row of *chinars*—the lovely oriental planes whose white filigree of stems pattern so dazzlingly in winter and early spring against the blue Persian sky.

In the lower galleries near the entrance to the Bazaars were the coffee-houses, which by seven or eight o'clock in the morning were already full of coffee-drinkers and tobacco-smokers. The guests sat in a circle, in the middle of which stood a large vessel of water for the cleaning of foul pipes. Abbas the Great, finding that the coffee-houses were becoming hotbeds of political intrigue, directed that a *mulla* should be in permanent attendance to deliver to these ' Tobacco-whiffers and Coffee-quaffers ' edifying lectures on history, poetry or the law.

Adjoining the coffee-houses were certain taverns which also served as brothels. At night the vaulted rooms, hung with lamps and candles, had, thought Herbert, ' a curious splendour '; often of an evening the Shah and his boon companions would come there for entertainment—' tumbling, sleight-of-hand, dancing girls and painted catamites (that *nefandum peccatum* being there tolerated) '.[32]

For those who merely sought food, rather than wine and other reprehensible pleasures, there were respectable restaurants; there were also tea-houses, equally respectable, whose clients played chess or a game that resembled *tric-trac*. Olearius considered that Persians played chess extremely well—even better than Russians, who were generally recognized, then as now, to be the best chess-players in Europe.

Since the Maidan served many different purposes, the image we attempt to revive must depend upon the occasion. Normally most of the twenty acres of the square were given over to the booths and tents of petty hucksters, grouped according to their trades, who spread out their wares on the ground; the space near the Ali Qapu was, however, always kept clear to preserve access to the Palace. In one corner melons, vegetables and dried fruit would be offered for sale; in other parts of the square squatted the sellers of leather and cotton goods, of silks and satins, of gums and drugs and spices, of wood and charcoal, of iron tools and bric-à-brac, of camels, horses and mules. Here were the book-binders, there the makers of trunks and boxes; and when trade with Europe developed, a special spot was reserved for the sale of trinkets from Nuremberg and Venice. On one day in the week peasants came in from the surrounding country with window-frames, doors, locks and keys,

23. Dome of the Lutfullah Mosque showing perhaps the most intricate tilework anywhere in Isfahan.

63

and other objects made in their villages. On occasions the order was given for the booths to be cleared away, so that the square could be used for polo or for some form of pageantry; but more often the stalls were left up all night, and so vigilant were the Police, so ruthless in their treatment of thieves, that nothing was ever stolen.

Besides the buyers and the sellers there were also, of course, the inevitable story-tellers, jugglers, mountebanks and acrobats, without whom no picture of an oriental market would seem complete. 'The wenches show a thousand tumbling tricks and

Fig. 11. Musicians Greeting the Dawn. (from *La Perse*, by Mme Dieulafoy, 1887).

antick postures', wrote Tavernier. 'When they have done, they come and ask the spectators for money, who give them every one what they think fit'.[33] He adds, 'They also have a sport at breaking of eggs, by knocking the ends one against another, some of which eggs come to three or four crowns'. For this variant of the children's games played in various part of Europe with chestnuts, eggs produced by a particularly sturdy race of cocks and hens were specially imported from a district several hundred miles from Isfahan.

In winter the Maidan was often under water, and mud in the streets was said to come up to the knees; but everyone of any importance—even shopkeepers—always went on horseback. In summer, men with watering cans laid the dust, which was never excessive because the ground was covered with fine river-sand. They also carried goatskins with iced water for the thirsty; and no charge was made for this distribution, charitable persons having endowed it in perpetuity.

To the general uproar of a great market square there was added, at certain times of the day and night, the cacophonous strains of a band of the kind that used to play in all oriental capitals, generally at sundown, to indicate the residence of royalty. Della Valle was almost the only European who found these compulsory concerts,

24. Young man in a garden. A miniature in the style of Muhammadi, *c.* A. D. 1580. *Treasury, Topkapi Palace Museum, Istanbul.*

64

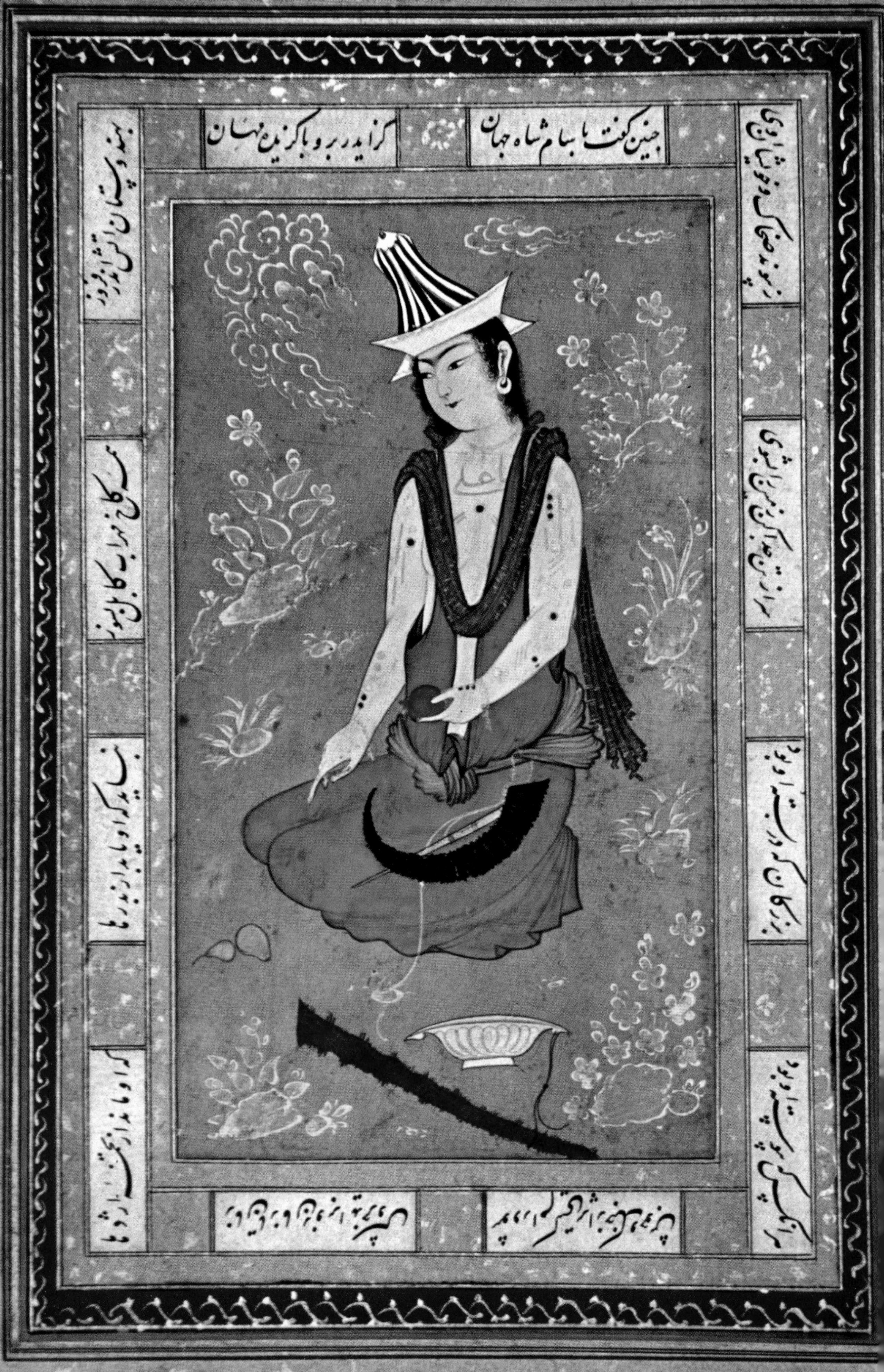

which were so noisy that they were audible all over the Maidan, pleasant to listen to; Thévenot voiced the more general opinion that they were more calculated to alarm than to entertain. This orchestra played from the upper galleries adjoining the entrance to the Royal Bazaar. The instruments used were ' tambours, trumpets, tymbals, clavecins, hautbois, drums, flutes, harps and cymbals '. The trumpets were more than eight feet long, and made in two pieces which screwed together; strength to hold them, rather than any peculiar musical talent, seems to have been the chief qualification for joining that particular section of the band.

Over the entrance to the Bazaar there was once a large clock which had been made for Abbas by an Englishman named ' Festy '. After Festy's death—it seems that he was murdered by a Persian—the clock stopped, and no one could be found who was capable of repairing it. Above the clock hung a big bronze bell, looted from a Portuguese nunnery at Hormuz, which bore the inscription *Sancta Maria, Ora Pro Nobis Mulieribus*. It was never sounded, and about the year 1800 was melted down for cannon. At roughly the same period the clock also disappeared. Loot from Hormuz also included about 120 guns, which were placed upon a low wall in front of the Ali Qapu.

Clocks of all kinds have always fascinated oriental potentates. To amuse the ten-year-old Abbas II when he came to the throne in 1642, there was set up, on the eastern side of the Maidan and just to the south of the Lutfullah Mosque, one of those elaborate clocks still found in Strasbourg and some other European cities. At the stroke of each hour a marionette show was performed by representations of human beings whose bodies were painted on a flat surface but whose heads, arms and legs were free to move. Each figure had its musical instrument, upon which it played with excruciating results; there were also birds and various other animals which fluttered about or joined in combat. Chardin considered it extremely crude and also very painful to the ears. This clock and its tower have long since vanished.

The mast in the middle of the Maidan served for archery practice. Upon the top of it was placed an apple or a small melon, a plate filled with silver, or—on royal occasions—a golden cup. The archers, riding at full gallop, had to pass the mast, then turn in the saddle to fire. Tavernier saw Shah Safi, a fine athlete, bring down three cups in five courses. The sport was a traditional one; Angiolello, when he was in Tabriz about the year 1510, watched Shah Ismail score seven hits in ten shots. At a later date the mast in Isfahan was replaced by an execution pole upon which the victim was suspended by his heels and either dashed to the ground or killed with a knife.

In the evenings the Maidan was often used for polo. The origins of this ancient oriental sport are lost in antiquity. The Sasanian monarchs played well and were hard hitters of the ball, though one may beg leave to doubt Firdausi's account of the prowess of Gushtasp, who was said to have struck the ball so vigorously that it disappeared into the clouds. In early days women also took part. The soldiers of Tamerlane invented a macabre variant of the game by using the heads of their enemies instead of balls. The Moghul Emperor Akbar, when selecting a minister, used to judge of his suitability by observing his behaviour on the polo ground; he also sometimes played by night, using lighted balls of slow-burning wood.

Abbas the Great would often invite a man of quite humble origin to join his team if he was known to show promise. He himself was an excellent player, as good as any man in his kingdom; it was reported of him that when he was about to make an unusually ferocious shot he would loudly invoke the name of Santiago, the patron saint of Spain whom the Persians, for some curious reason, identified with the Caliph Ali. Whenever Abbas hit the ball, the trumpeters in the gallery by the entrance to the Bazaar acknowledged his achievement by sounding a fanfare. When the Shah was not himself playing, he usually watched from the balcony of the Ali

25. A dervish shown with his horn and begging bowl.
A miniature in the style of Riza Abbasi, *c.* A. D. 1620.
Treasury, Topkapi Museum. Istanbul.

Qapu, drinking cup upon cup of snow-chilled Shiraz wine with his courtiers. But he also had a little ' house on wheels ', drawn by oxen, in which he could be rushed to whatever part of the ground was seeing the best of the play.

Della Valle gives a detailed account of polo as it appeared to a European un-familiar with the game. He thought it rather like the Florentine *calcio* (football), but less rough and altogether nobler. It reminded Figueroa, the Spanish Ambassador, of a kind of hockey played (but on foot) by Spanish peasants. The polo players did not wear uniform, but their ' fantastic coats of various colours, with rich plumed turbans and the like ', made a brave show, and the effect was ' quite military '.

' The King comes often abroad in the evening to see lions, bears, bulls, rams, cocks, and all other sorts of creatures fight ', wrote Tavernier. ' The sport itself is poor ', thought Della Valle, ' but the joyful sound of several thousand people running, leaping, shouting, laughing, and waving their cloaks, all at the same moment, is very exhilarating and enjoyable '.

The animals which were used for these and other sports were kept in a small zoo in the Palace grounds, near the royal stables, which several Europeans managed to visit. Chardin, writing at a rather later date, was deeply impressed by the rhi-noceros—a considerable rarity in captivity at that time—which had been brought to Isfahan by an Ethiopian ambassador as a gift from his master to Shah Abbas II. In his *Voyages* Chardin describes the animal in great detail and gives a drawing of it which compares favourably with Dürer's more famous woodcut of the Lisbon rhi-noceros, made in 1515 after the sketch of a friend. Chardin wrote that the rhi-noceros was kept in a den with two elephants, with which it seemed to live in com-plete harmony—' and I also saw, on several occasions, the three of them together in the Maidan, without any sign of mutual antipathy '.

It is Fryer [34] who gives us the fullest account of the royal zoo, whose inmates had, he considered, more freedom than the ladies of the royal harem. He also, of course, describes the rhinoceros, and adds that although there is normally ' a mortal strife ' between elephant and rhinoceros, the captive specimen was successfully ' kept facing two mighty, but lean elephants '. Another attraction was the zebras, also a present from the Emperor of Ethiopia. In addition, there were bears, leopards and lions, and some remarkable birds including a number of freaks which Fryer describes in detail. Fryer also speaks of hawking. The best hawks, he says, came from Russia and were extremely expensive to buy. Persian hawks were ' a cowardly breed ... teaching the crows of the country to be too hard for them '. For hunting, the Per-sian greyhound was excellent, and Malcolm [35] describes antelope-hunting with them. There were also English mastiffs, always a popular gift for an English ambassador to bring to an oriental monarch.

Another event which began and ended in the Maidan was the cross-country race held periodically for those who wanted to qualify as *shatirs* or ' runners '. Every rich man had his *shatirs*, who were trained from an early age to cover enormous distances in a day. When these tests were due to be held, the master set up a starting-post in the Maidan, and there entertained his friends with a picnic meal and dancing girls. The *shatirs*, their legs smeared with grease, went naked but for a pair of drawers supported by a belt hung with small bells. They had to run backwards and forwards between the Maidan and a stone about four or five miles outside the town. The route was carefully patrolled to prevent cheating, and at the stone was an official who, each time a *shatir* arrived at it, gave him an arrow to carry back to the starting-post where the dancing girls, like seconds in a boxing ring, were waiting to massage him and urge him on to yet greater effort. With no more sustenance than an occasional sip of sherbet, a good *shatir* could run more than a hundred miles between sunrise and sunset.

26. The Thirty-three-arch Bridge (early seventeenth century).

26

Abbas the builder

To DISCUSS FURTHER the daily life of the court and of the people of Isfahan without first describing the appearance of the city in which they lived and moved, would be to set the action in a vacuum. In fact, in order to give a picture of the activities of the Maidan, we have been obliged to depict the great square as it appeared towards the close of the reign of Abbas the Great, when the principal buildings that surround it had been more or less completed. We must now turn back to the year 1600, when there was little to be seen beyond the small Timurid palace and the vast open space—possibly already in use as a market—around which Abbas's buildings were soon to spring up.

ALI QAPU

Most probably the first task to be undertaken was the transformation of the little Timurid palace into the Ali Qapu, or 'Sublime Porte'—at once a lodging, a grandstand, an audience chamber, and a state gateway leading to the Palace grounds. As soon as it was ready, Abbas made it his headquarters while his architects began the creation, under his direction and often under his personal supervision, of his new capital.

The original palace had been squat; Abbas raised it by three storeys and extended it to provide the great covered balcony (talar) [36] commanding a view of the Maidan. The ground floor was made over to the officers of the guard, the upper floors being reserved for the Shah's private use. There is some justification for Robert Byron's jibe at 'that brick boot-box'; at all events it could not be described as great architecture, yet it takes its place agreeably enough in the backcloth of the Maidan.

Certainly the interior is enchanting, if rather whimsical. Most of the rooms are small and homely, and Abbas must have enjoyed their informality as did the French kings their Trianons and petits appartements. Although much of the decoration has fallen into decay, and innumerable repaintings and restorations have been undertaken at various times, what is visible today gives at any rate some impression of the original appearance. Herbert states that the rooms were decorated in red, white, blue and gold, the walls painted with landscapes and hunting scenes, the floors covered with carpets of silk and gold. Today the floors are bare, the overall decorations low in tone, soft in colour, and so small in pattern that they suggest printed cottons or Victorian wall-papers. In the upper rooms are figure compositions of quite a different kind and these are discussed by Della Valle.

To one accustomed to Italian Mannerist art, Persian figure painting seemed incompetent and ill-drawn, and Della Valle was much afraid that if Abbas were to see the pictures of the European artist who was working for him, the man would be taken into the service of the Shah. The subjects of these figure paintings in the Ali Qapu are mildly erotic, but no more so than those of a Boucher or a Fragonard.

27. *Ivan* of the Royal Mosque (early seventeenth century).

71

All these pictures [wrote Della Valle] show men and women in lascivious postures. Some stand with flagons of wine and cups in their hands; others lie asleep in a drunken stupor; yet others are reeling as the wine goes to their heads:—pictures, that is to say, of Bacchus and Venus united. Among these figures, which are mostly dressed in the costume of the country, are a number wearing hats and intended to represent Europeans; apparently they are designed to show that Persians are not the only people addicted to wine...

The Italian did, however, have praise for the richness of the colours used. At the time of his visit the decorations were still incomplete. At some stage, European artists—most probably Dutchmen—contributed to them.

The *piano nobile* of the Ali Qapu consists of the delightfully decorated throne-room, and the *talar* with its slender wooden columns, russet-coloured roof, and rectangular, jasper-bordered pool. The water for the pool used to be raised by means of hydraulic machines worked by oxen, but today it stands empty. From here, precipitous winding staircases lead finally to the music room at the very top of the building, whose walls and ceilings are curiously pierced (as if fret-sawed), in the shapes of flagons and wine-vessels. Chardin tells us that these niches were filled with vessels of glass, pottery, enamelled metal and semi-precious stones, but it is probable that they were also intended to improve the acoustics. Open porches, similarly decorated, surround the music room, and these are provided with fire-places for winter use. The view of the Maidan from the upper storeys is magnificent, particularly at sunset.

In Safavid times, peculiar sanctity was attached to the main gateway of the Ali Qapu. No one was allowed to walk over the threshold, and even the Shah dismounted to pass through. All who sought the royal favour kissed the gate, which was considered *bast* (asylum) for criminals and fugitives; the Shah himself could not drag a man from it except by starvation.

Thévenot mentions a sacred stone which appears to have been in the alley leading from the Ali Qapu, and Tavernier adds some further details:

It is the custom of all Ambassadors to salute the Gate of Ali by reason of a white marble stone made like an ass's back, and which serves for a step; being, as they report, brought anciently out of Arabia, where Ali lived. That day the new King receives his insignia of royalty, he goes to stride over the stone, and if by negligence he should chance to touch it, there are four guards at the gate that would make a show of thrusting him back again.[37]

There was indeed a legend that Abbas had brought the entire gateway from the tomb of Ali at Nejef; neither ' Gate of Ali ' nor ' Gate of God ' (*Allah Qapu*), but ' Sublime Porte ' is, however, the correct reading of the name.

THE CHAHAR BAGH

The Chahar Bagh, the Champs Elysées of Isfahan, was designed by Abbas to be the grand approach to his new capital. The name, which means ' four gardens ', is derived from the four vineyards that originally occupied the site.

It might very naturally be imagined that Abbas would have made his avenue lead directly to the Maidan; in fact it came to an end at a point west of the Palace grounds, where a pavilion had been erected for the royal seraglio to survey the scene. It was, indeed, as much a promenade as an avenue in this upper section; in the other direction, after crossing the river it became a thoroughfare leading to the royal gardens of Hazarjarib and to Julfa.

Abbas's design was this. Down the centre of the avenue flowed a canal, with water dropping in little cascades from terrace to terrace and now and again arrested in big rectangular or octagonal basins edged with onyx. In the summer months these tanks were filled with cut heads of roses which floated on the surface of the water. Then, on either side of the canal, came a row of *chinars*, a promenade, parterres filled with shrubs and flowers, and finally a further row of *chinars*. The total breadth was about fifty yards. Chardin informs us that Abbas would allow no tree to be planted when he was not present, and that under every tree was buried a gold and a silver coin of his reign.

Beside the Chahar Bagh, open archways led to further gardens and pavilions. There were the Gardens of the Throne, the Nightingale, the Vineyard, the Mulberries, the Dervishes, and so on. Some of these pavilions were used as coffee-houses, and of an evening the Chahar Bagh was always thronging with life. Fryer wrote that at nightfall all the ' pride ' of Isfahan gathered there ' and the Grandees were airing themselves, prancing about with their numerous trains, striving to outvie each other in pomp and generosity '. No doubt Olearius was justified in calling the Chahar Bagh ' one of the most beautiful and charming spots in the world '.

It is no longer easy to visualize the Chahar Bagh as it must have appeared in the days of Abbas, though written descriptions abound and several of the early travel books contain engravings of it. But in 1840, when the great rows of plane trees had reached full maturity, Flandin and Coste made two attractive lithographs which give a very clear picture of the promenade as it then was. Soon after this, however, decay set in. Lord Curzon, after describing the Chahar Bagh in its heyday, continues:

> But now [1892] what a tragical contrast! The channels are empty, their stone borders crumbled and shattered, the terraces are broken down, the parterres are unsightly bare patches, the trees, all lopped and pollarded, have been chipped and hollowed out or cut down for fuel by the soldiery of the Zil, the side pavilions are abandoned and crumbling to pieces, and the gardens are wildernesses. Two centuries of decay could never make the Champs Elysées in Paris, the Unter den Linden in Berlin, or Rotten Row in London, look one half as miserable as does the ruined avenue of Shah Abbas. It is in itself an epitome of modern Iran.[38]

THE RIVER

The Zayandeh-rud separates Isfahan from its southern suburbs, which include Julfa and what in Safavid times was the Zoroastrian settlement of Guebristan. The river rises in the Zagros mountains to the west of Isfahan, irrigates the Isfahan oasis, then vanishes in the salt marshes of Gav-Khaneh in the direction of Yazd. From the same range of the Zagros, the 12,500-foot peaks of the Kuh-i-rang, the impetuous Karun river flows southwards through Shushtar and Ahwaz to the Persian Gulf.

The Safavid Shahs made strenuous efforts to divert a part of the abundant waters of the Karun to swell the feeble flow of the Zayandeh-rud. Tahmasp began to excavate a tunnel at Kar Kunan, but foul air put a stop to the work. Abbas the Great attempted a cutting, at moments (according to Herbert) employing no less than 100,000 men; but he was defeated by ice and snow. Abbas II engaged a French engineer, a man named Genest, to mine rock and build dams to raise the level of the Zayandeh-rud. But all these projects came to naught.

The unfinished cutting, a huge cleft sawn across the crest of the mountain, can still be seen; it probably represents less than a twentieth part of what was necessary. Yet the scheme was perfectly rational; it was merely that it was beyond the powers of seventeenth-century engineering. Curzon maintained that in his day it would have presented no difficulties, but that the Shah was about as unlikely to undertake a genuinely great public work as he was to turn Protestant. At long last something was done: in 1953 a tunnel was cut which increases the flow of the Zayandeh-rud by a minimum of thirty cubic yards per second. For much of the year, however, the river still makes but a poor showing in its wide bed, and in Isfahan in high summer and autumn is often totally dry; in general, only when the mountain snows melt in the spring does it become a river in the true sense of the word.

Five bridges cross the river in or around Isfahan. The oldest of these, the Shahristan, has already been described (p. 28). Two of the Safavid bridges—the Allahverdi Khan, and the Khwaju (built under Abbas II)—rank among the finest architectural achievements of the dynasty. Curzon, not given to unconsidered praise, says of the former that it is alone worth a visit to Isfahan to see what may, in all probability, be termed the most stately bridge in the world. Even Tavernier, quick enough to find fault, conceded that it was 'a very neat piece of architecture, if I may not say the neatest in all Persia'.

The Allahverdi Khan bridge, more commonly known as the Si-u-seh-pul or 'Thirty-three (arch) bridge', was built soon after the year 1600, to connect the town with Julfa and with the royal gardens of Hazarjarib or 'Thousand Acres'. Allahverdi Khan, who had it constructed, was Governor-General of Fars and Abbas's most trusted Commander-in-Chief. Every traveller who visited Isfahan has described its complicated and ingenious design. Its piers and towers are of stone, the upper part of brick; its length is more than 300 yards, its breadth about 15 yards. On either side of the roadway there is a covered arcade, inconveniently low, pierced internally and externally by nearly a hundred small pointed arches and interrupted by several pavilions. Above and below these arcades are further promenades, so that the bridge could be crossed on foot on three different levels.

THE SHAIKH LUTFULLAH MOSQUE

From the river we return to the Maidan, where in 1603 Abbas began the construction of a small but enchantingly beautiful building, the Masjid-i-Shaikh Lutfullah. The Shaikh, as every writer on Isfahan informs us, was 'the saintly father-in-law' of Shah Abbas and the most famous preacher of his day.

Most, if not all, early travellers to Isfahan failed to gain an entry into the Lutfullah Mosque, and in general they dismiss it with hardly a mention. Chardin describes the interior in some detail, but he probably obtained his information at second hand. He called the Mosque 'gloomy, and little used'; no doubt the greater size and obvious brilliance of the Royal Mosque made a more immediate appeal. But even among those who could not enter the Lutfullah, the magnificent tile-work and Yazd marble steps of the entrance portal, and the restrained beauty of the dome, might have been expected to excite more interest and more praise.

Externally the dome, both in form and in colour, is unusual. The form is squat and the dominant colour and surface of the tile-work is not a glittering blue but an unglazed *café-au-lait*. The arabesques are glazed white, turquoise and deep blue, sweeping in majestic curves across the buff ground, and there is a good deal of blue in the drum. Very skilful use has been made of this contrast between glazed and unglazed tiles, which gives a fitful glitter to the surface as the sunlight strikes it. Looking across from the Ali Qapu, the dome and portal are seen reflected in the pool which has been constructed in the middle of the Maidan; and though in some ways it is hard not to regret the transformation of the great open polo ground into a garden, this mirrored image in the golden light of evening is of unforgettable beauty.

It soon becomes apparent to the spectator that the dome does not rise directly over the portal, but at a point rather to the south of it. This asymmetry is said, by several authors, to have been occasioned by the necessity for reconciling the south-west alignment of the *mihrab* with the north-south direction of the Maidan. But the

28. One of the side courts of the Royal Mosque (early seventeenth century).

Lutfullah, unlike the Royal Mosque, has no court and therefore presents no serious problem of orientation. The corridor leading from the portal to the interior of the Mosque turns a sharp corner, so that the entrance into the chamber is at a point precisely opposite the *mihrab*; but this could have been achieved without the displacement of the dome. One would prefer to think that symmetry, which was the tyranny of renaissance architects, did not trouble the Persians; at all events, the arrangement, for whatever reason it was adopted, adds greatly to the charm of the silhouette of the Lutfullah as seen across the Maidan.

' If the outside is lyrical, the inside is Augustan ', wrote Byron. His whole description of the Lutfullah is, indeed, among the most brilliant passages in a brilliant book.[39] Within, the dome is an inverted saucer, suspended above a battery of little windows which shed a rather wan light upon the interior. The structure is simple: the square of the ground-plan develops effortlessly into the circle of the drum which supports the dome. But if the form is simple, the decoration is of incredible richness. As Byron says, Versailles, the porcelain rooms at Schönbrunn, the Doge's Palace, St Peter's, are rich, but this surpasses them all in sheer exuberance of decoration. Blue predominates in the tile-work, but there is an unusual amount of buff; and, as in the exterior, there is the flickering contrast between glazed and unglazed tiles. Nowhere in Islamic architecture can calligraphy have been more dramatically used, the texts being in white on a ground of midnight blue; it is the work of Ali Reza, the greatest calligrapher of his day.

Yet for all the wonder of colour and arabesque, for all the glitter of tile-work and nobility of form, the interior of the Lutfullah is strangely enervating. There comes upon the spectator a feeling of claustrophobia, of being sunk in some blue ocean lit only by moonlight filtered through deep waters. It is with something of a sense of release that he emerges into the sunshine and the fresh air of the Maidan.

THE MAQSUD BEG AND SURKHI MOSQUES

Two other mosques date from the opening years of the seventeenth century—the Maqsud Beg (or Zuleimat) and the Surkhi.

Maqsud Beg was Royal Steward to Abbas the Great, and a very wealthy man. It was Abbas's habit to visit the rich and suggest that they should erect, at their own expense, a building that would enhance the beauty and prestige of his capital. Such suggestions were, needless to say, tantamount to commands. Thus Maqsud Beg came to build, in 1601-2, the Mosque which still bears his name. A pleasant building with a fine tiled portal, it stands beside the Khiaban-i-Hafiz, close to the northeast corner of the Maidan. Within is a domed chamber with a *mihrab* bearing an inscription written by Ali Reza, and a smaller chamber containing the tomb of his calligraphic rival and sworn enemy, Mir Imad.

The Surkhi Mosque was built in 1605-6 by Khalaf, the Shah's ' Sufreji ' (*Maître d'Hôtel*); in the course of time *sufreji* has become *surkhi*, the Persian for ' red '. Today it is stripped of its tile-work and is only of interest to the antiquarian.

THE ROYAL MOSQUE (MASJID-I-SHAH)

The second phase of Abbas's building programme opened in 1611/12 with the consolidation of the Maidan, and the following year work began on the Royal Mosque, the largest and the most spectacular monument of his reign.[40]

Abbas had now been on the throne for twenty-five years, and though he was still

29. North-east *ivan* of the Royal Mosque.

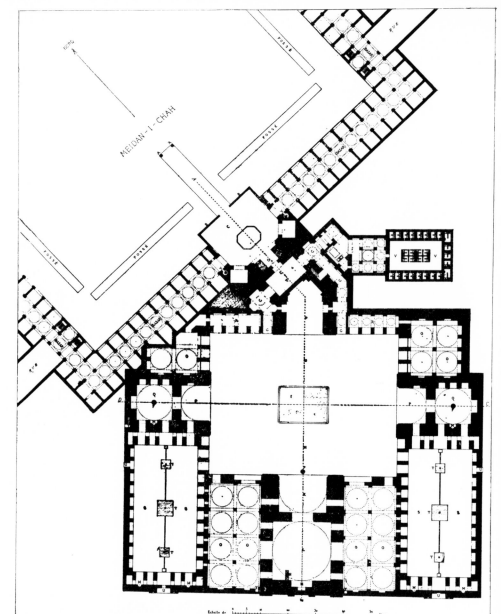

A Grey limestone polo goal-
    posts
B Low wall marking bound-
    ary of precinct
C Portal of the Mosque
D Main entrance
E Vestibule
F Drinking fountain
G Entrances to the Mosque
H Main court, paved with
    flagstones
I Pool for ablutions
K Portal of the Sanctuary
L Sanctuary and main dome
M Niches indicating direction
    of prayer
N Pulpit
O Prayer rooms
P Ivans
Q Domed chambers
R Porticoes
S Paved courts
T Pools and fountains
V Latrines
X Water tank
Y Stairs to galleries and roof

Fig. 12. Ground Plan of the Royal Mosque (from *Monuments Modernes de la Perse*, by Pascal Coste, 1867).

30. Street scene showing the dome
and minarets
of the Royal Mosque
in the background.

31. Entrance portal
to the Royal Mosque
(early seventeenth century).

in his early forties he must have felt that the time that remained to him might well prove too short for the completion of his capital. His architects were therefore driven hard, and inevitably construction became shoddy and foundations ill-prepared. Even among his earlier buildings there were signs of over-haste: the Thirty-three-arch bridge and the Maqsud Beg Mosque today show more cracks and subsidence than many a Seljuq building of the twelfth century, and the Lutfullah Mosque has caused much anxiety to those architects and experts whose duty it is to preserve the national monuments of Isfahan. Abbas also wanted to save time and money by removing Yazd marble from the Friday Mosque, but fortunately

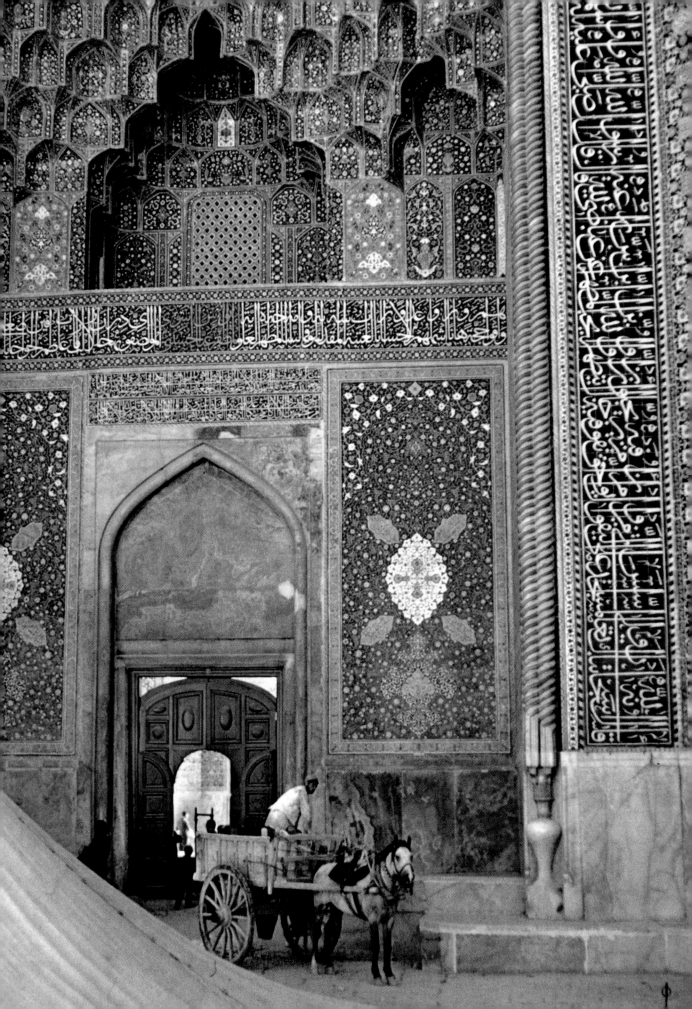

32

34

33

the *mullas* were able to persuade him that creating such a precedent might one day result in his own Mosque being similarly desecrated.

An important but unsatisfactory labour-saving innovation was the *haft-rangi* tile. Timurid and early Safavid tile-work was true tile-mosaic: each tile was of one colour only, precisely cut to fill its allotted space. The *haft-rangi* (' seven-colour ') tile was usually square, and combined a number of different colours in a single firing. Far quicker and far cheaper to make and to fit in place, it served the purpose of swiftly covering a wall with colour; but it lacked the brilliance of the more laborious mosaic. In the portal of the Royal Mosque, and indeed in the Lutfullah Mosque also, the two types of tile-work may be seen side by side, and no one who compares the two techniques can fail to appreciate the greater merits of true tile-mosaic.

The portal of the Royal Mosque was finished in 1616, at which time the Mosque itself had probably advanced little further than the foundation; no doubt Abbas was eager to complete the southern façade of the Maidan before undertaking the far greater project of the Mosque itself. Though there may be more delicacy of tile-work, more ingenuity of arabesque, more richness of colour in the portals of several other Persian mosques, it is hard to recall any which is more dramatic in impact or more wholly satisfying as an *ensemble*. The scale is immense (though the portal of the Shrine of the Imam Reza at Meshed is still loftier), the arch being almost ninety feet in height. There is, too, added mystery from the almost perpetual shadow which envelops this north-facing portal. Yet though it is mysterious it is by no means gloomy, for the tiles glitter with the light reflected from the sun-filled Maidan and the white walls which enclose it.

The arch itself is framed by a triple cable ornament, rich turquoise in colour and rising from large marble ' vases '. The semi-dome is filled with clustering stalactites, and on each side of the actual entrance hang two great tiled panels like prayer carpets. Flanking the portal, and cutting across the corners of the rectangular area which gives access to it, are two niches containing reduced versions of the stalactite decoration of the semi-dome of the main portal.

Much more remains to be mentioned. There is the relief of heraldic peacocks above the little central door—a motif which occurs in the Shrines at Ardebil and Meshed and which must have had some special, though no longer ascertainable, significance. There is the pool, which so splendidly echoes the rich intricacy of the tile-work. There are the two minarets, 110 feet in height, which dominate the façade. There are the doors themselves, which Shah Safi covered with silver plates. And there is the great calligraphic frieze, the work of Ali Reza and dated 1616, that proclaims the glory of God and of Shah Abbas.

All this is but the prelude to the Mosque itself, whose ' huge blue bulk and huge acreage of coarse floral tilework ' were dismissed by Robert Byron as constituting ' just that kind of " oriental " scenery, so dear to the Omar Khayam fiends—pretty, if you like, even magnificent, but not important in the general scale of things '. But the visitor can hardly fail to be astonished when he enters the great court. (This entry is effected by means of a half-right turn, made so that the alignment of the court, and thus of the *mihrab*, may point towards Mecca. The bending of this monumental building ' without any sense of fracture or discrepancy ' is a triumph of architectural ingenuity and skill.)

The court follows the typical pattern of the Persian four-*ivan* mosque; its immediate inspiration is undoubtedly the Gauhar Shad Mosque at Meshed. Its four sides are walled with two-storeyed arcades broken in the centres by towering portals, the largest of which, that in the south-west façade, leads to the Sanctuary. Over the Sanctuary rises the huge turquoise dome—the dome which first greets the traveller as he approaches Isfahan.

32. Julfa Cathedral showing its free-standing belfry, dates from the first half of the seventeenth century.

33. Royal Mosque. Detail of the entrance portal (early seventeenth century).

34. Royal Mosque entrance portal.

The tile-work which covers every square inch of the interior of the court lacks the richness of mosaic faience; it has, however, a softness of tone, a texture, that is almost powdery and which has its own particular charm. The overall colour of the façades is the pastel-blue of love-in-a-mist, not the gentian blue of Timurid tile-work. And perhaps it is just as well that these enormous areas of wall are not too glittering; the eye would be dazzled by such an acreage of intense colour.

Two further minarets surmount the *ivan* which leads to the Sanctuary. The interior of the Sanctuary has been described as ' almost too well lit for the deepest mood '; none the less it is exciting and magnificent. The ceiling of the dome is dominated by a dramatic medallion such as is often to be found in the carpets of north-western Iran. On each side of the Sanctuary are oratories where the same motif occurs in the domical vaults. Beyond these oratories are two further courts, more intimate in character, each with its pool. It has been estimated that 18 million bricks and half a million tiles were used in the building of the Masjid-i-Shah. The figures are enormous, yet not improbable.

One or two early travellers seem to have succeeded in entering the main court of the mosque. Thévenot did so in the time of Abbas II.

> Christians are not allowed to enter it [he wrote] and if anyone is found there and recognized, he is driven out with cudgels like a dog; yet that did not prevent my going there with Monsieur Diager, the master of the Dutch factory at Ispahan. For the purpose we both put on native dress, and were not molested in any way.

Probably until the nineteenth century no Christian advanced farther than the main Court, and Curzon (in 1890) knew of only two—J. S. Buckingham (in 1816) and F. Flandin (in 1840)—who had succeeded in getting into the remaining parts of the mosque. Flandin was able to make an accurate plan of the whole building—a plan which Mme Dieulafoy made unacknowledged use of in her book. Curzon mentions that the two side-courts were in his day open to ' the public ' on Fridays, but it is not clear whether he refers to Christian, or only to Moslem, visitors. Access is now unimpeded for most of the day, though the prayers of the faithful must, very naturally, be respected; but in the seventeenth century the mosques of Isfahan must have presented the same obstacles to the Christian as those of Qum and Meshed still do today.[41]

THE BAZAARS

At the northern end of the Maidan stands the Qaisariyeh, or ' Royal Bazaar ', and the labyrinth of smaller bazaars which beyond it run like a rabbit warren through the heart of the old town. The portal of the Qaisariyeh was built at about the same time as that of the Royal Mosque, which it confronts and in a sense echoes; Della Valle mentions seeing it in 1617. Above the archway is a badly damaged mural representing Abbas the Great battling with the Özbegs.

Such are the principal buildings of Abbas's reign. In the short space of a single generation, Isfahan had been transformed. In Europe, town-planning was at this time no novelty; but in Asia it was usual for a city to sprawl haphazardly round its Friday Mosque, as had the medieval cities of Europe round their cathedrals or castles. Abbas the Great was a pioneer in his conception of an ordered eastern metropolis—a metropolis more than able to stand comparison with the finest cities in Christendom. It is only in the present century that the attempt has been made, by the construction of a ' grid ' of broad avenues (still uncompleted), to carry Abbas's scheme to its logical conclusion.

35. Yellow-glazed earthenware ewer (seventeenth century). *Victoria and Albert Museum*, London.

36. *Haft-rangi* tile mosaic, period of Shah Abbas. *Victoria and Albert Museum, London.*

Life in Isfahan

WHEN JOHN CHARDIN, the Huguenot traveller and jeweller, was in Isfahan in 1666 he decided to collect material for a full description of the city and its buildings. In this task he was much helped by a highly intelligent and knowledgeable Dutch merchant named Herbert Diager, and by two *mullas*. Ten years later Chardin sorted and arranged the large amount of material that had accumulated, and the resultant work constitutes volume VIII of the ten-volume edition of his Travels, and is the most important survey of Isfahan in the seventeenth century.

This volume, together with volumes V, VI and VII, also gives us a full picture of the Persians and their way of life—of education, government and religion; of food and drink, inns and public baths; of their houses and their family life; of their sports, festivals, pastimes and trades. Since most of Chardin's time was spent in the capital, it is of the Isfahanis that he principally writes. And though he deals with Isfahan in the 1660s and 1670s, his account will serve us for a description of life in the town in the days of Abbas the Great.

THE PEOPLE

Chardin considered the Persians a handsome people, but only because of a generous infusion of foreign blood; 'There is hardly a gentleman in Persia', he wrote, 'whose mother is not a Georgian or a Circassian'. He found them well-bred, amusing, amiable, civil, intelligent, and extremely hospitable. They had remarkably good memories and a great natural aptitude for learning. They were, he affirmed, the most civilized of all Orientals with whom he had come into contact. But their vices were as numerous and as apparent as their virtues. They were idle, wanton, corrupt, double-faced, and reckless where money was concerned. 'In short, they are born with as good potentials as any other people, but few abuse them to such an extent'.

The Persian house was built of mud or sun-dried brick, the soil being heavy enough to make such a structure reasonably solid and durable. In the centre was a court-yard, and often each separate room was covered with a dome to save the use of wood. Water, rather than fire, was the principal danger to be feared. Chardin adds the curious information that the brick-layers wore gloves so as to avoid soiling the bricks with the sweat of their hands, and that where timber was used, salt was spread upon it to keep it free from worm.

The women of course remained much at home, and probably the most eventful moments of the week would be the visit to the mosque and to the *hammam* (public bath). Of these baths there was an enormous number in the city—the Royal, the White, the Paradise, the Thursday, the Stone-cutters' Hammam, and so on. Many were erected as speculative ventures by private individuals, or were attached to mosques or madrasehs which were in part supported by their takings.

In general the Persians ate less than the Europeans. Chardin suggests several reasons for this: the hotter climate; their dislike of taking exercise; the lack of variety in their food and the absence of wine and spirits to stimulate an appetite; and the excessive smoking of tobacco and opium.

37. Mural painting
in the Chihil Sutun
(seventeenth century).

Fig. 13. Pigeon Towers at Isfahan (from *La Perse*, by Mme Dieulafoy, 1887).

The day started early with a hunk of bread and a cup of coffee, to be followed at mid-morning by fruit, curds and sweetmeats. The principal meal came at about seven in the evening, with egg dishes, kebab or pilau—all prepared very simply and without the use of spices. To drink there were sherbets of various kinds. The poor did not cook at home, but purchased their food already prepared from one or other of the many cook-shops, or communal kitchens, in the town.

The fruit of Isfahan—especially its melons—has always been famous. During the season many of the poor lived almost entirely on melons and cucumbers, eating in a single day more than did the French in a whole month, and Chardin records that a man could eat thirty-five pounds of fruit at a single meal without ill effects. This high consumption of fruit was generally believed to be very healthy; the story is told of two itinerant doctors who arrived in Isfahan with the intention of settling there, but who hastily packed up their bags and left the town when they saw the quantities of fruit in the shops. The innumerable pigeon-towers (Chardin mentions that in his day there were some 3000 of them), whose remains are still visible all around the town, provided manure for the melon fields, and the finest fruit was stored in ice-houses so that it might be available all the year round for those who could afford it. Since the annual rainfall of Isfahan is only about four or five inches, extensive irrigation was necessary to produce all this excellent fruit.

Over-indulgence in tobacco-smoking, especially among the upper classes, became a serious problem in the seventeenth century, and Abbas the Great himself gave up smoking to set an example. When this failed, he had horse-dung substituted for tobacco in the *qalians* (hubble-bubbles) which were set before his courtiers, who thought it politic to praise it as the best tobacco they had ever tried. ' Then the Shah turned and, looking angrily at them all, said, " Cursed be the drug that cannot be distinguished from horse-dung! " ' Opium, taken in a variety of ways, was used by all classes of the community, but only ' the scum of the people ' resorted to In-

38. Youth with a cockerel, a miniature painted by Muin Musavvir (third quarter of the seventeenth century). *Treasury, Topkapi Palace Museum, Istanbul.*

39

40 41

dian hemp. There was also a good deal of drinking, openly at court and on the sly elsewhere, of wine supplied by the Armenians in Julfa.

Chardin had the highest opinion of the Persian police:

> If anything is stolen, by day or by night, in the open country or at a caravanserai, the Governor of the Province is obliged either to recover the missing articles or refund a sum of money equivalent to their value. This was strictly carried out until towards the end of the reign of Abbas II, when after several very substantial thefts by highwaymen there was a good deal of deceit and procrastination. But the law still exists ...[42]

Thus, at least during the first half of the seventeenth century, the main roads were far safer than those of Europe, and robbers had a healthy respect for the efficiency of the royal archers who patrolled them.

There were no prisons in Isfahan, and justice was summary. Chardin considered that the Persian treatment of prisoners was

> ... gentle and humane compared with ours. In fact, our people are so depraved that if we did not deal with crime more harshly than they do in Persia, our towns and countryside would be be overrun by cut-throats ... In Persia you hardly ever hear of a house being broken into and its occupants murdered ... The whole time I was in Persia I only saw one man executed, so that all I have to tell about tortures there is only from hearsay.[43]

Government in general was surprisingly humane

> ... far beyond anything that might be expected of a despotic government with arbitrary powers. For instance, is there any other country where taxes and duties are so light? The people pay no capital tax, and all the necessities of life are tax-free. Could anything be more humane and kindly than the treatment of the peasants? One could call it a real partnership between landlord and serf, where profit and loss are shared equally and where the poor are always those who suffer the least.[44]

The army was well paid, so that the soldiers did not live off the land (as in Europe) and rob the peasants. In brief

> ... this is the most flourishing and most contented empire in the world ... I always think that a good way of judging the mildness of a government is to take a look at the lot of its inhabitants, particularly the lower orders. In Persia, both in the country and in the towns, these are well fed and well clothed, having all the household goods they need; and yet they do not work the half so hard as ours do. The poorest women have silver ornaments on their arms, feet and neck, and some wear gold coins....[45]

Those Isfahanis who found employment in the royal workshops seem to have fared best of all. There were thirty-two of these *ateliers* in the Palace grounds, and every kind of art and craft, from tailoring to clock-making, was carried on there. The men employed in them were expected to give only one-fifth of their time to the court; they were therefore able to earn plenty of extra money from private commissions. They were not dismissed when they became too old or too ill to work, but were allowed to retire on full wages and given free medical attention.

In Europe it was widely believed that the Persian peasant was a slave. This was quite untrue: he had complete freedom of movement. He could leave the country if he so wished, taking his family and all his possessions with him.

> There is also one inestimable advantage that these people have over ours: they are not harassed over religious matters. Their priests are neither numerous enough, rich enough, influential enough, nor sufficiently given to intrigue, to torment the people over religion. I do not mean that people are at liberty to start a new cult, or to become Christians or idolators openly. I simply mean that they are not forced to go to the mosques or persecuted if they hold unorthodox opinions. Everybody has complete freedom to believe what he chooses; so long as he does not publicly reject the Koran, he can interpret its mysteries as he sees fit.[46]

It was the upper stratum of society—the ministers and the court officials (of whom there was no end)—who had the most to fear, for without exception the Safavid

39. Helmet of Shah Abbas.
British Museum, London.

40. Armour of Shah Abbas.
British Museum, London.

41. Brass ewer
(early seventeenth century).
Victoria and Albert Museum, London.

Shahs were capricious and in their cups unpredictable and brutal. After all, there was much to be gained from the death of a rich man.

> I remember one day a lord named Rustam Khan coming to see me just after he had left the Shah [wrote Chardin]. He entered cheerfully, took out a pocket mirror and smilingly adjusted his turban. 'Every time I come away from the royal presence', he said, 'I take a look to see if my head is still on my shoulders ...'[47]

The Festival of Husain

Under the Safavids, that branch of Islam known as the Shi'a became the official religion of Iran.[48] The Shi'ites (as opposed to the Sunnis) hold that Muhammad's rightful successors were his son-in-law Ali, and Ali's descendants; they reject the elected Caliphs as usurpers and unorthodox. In general, Shi'ism was less strict in its observances than Sunnism.

For all Shi'ites, the great occasion of the year was the Festival of Husain, Muhammad's grandson, who had been killed at the Battle of Karbala and whose blood-stained shirt is still preserved in the Royal Mosque at Isfahan. Tavernier calls it a 'feast'; it could be better described as a ten days' fast culminating in a parade and finally a riot.

During the fast, nothing but lamentation could be heard in the streets. Black clothes were *de rigueur*; no one shaved, no one bathed; the sex life of the city came, theoretically, to a standstill. The more devout Muslims carried self-mortification still further. Some dug holes in the streets, buried themselves up to their necks and covered their heads with an old pot; they did not forget, however, to bring along a friend with a collecting-box. Others painted themselves black or red and ran naked through the city, howling, dancing, and beating time with bone castanets. In the mosques and at street corners *mullas* preached interminably on the theme of Husain's death, to audiences 'bathed in tears, sighing and moaning'.

The tenth day was the actual anniversary of Husain's death. Tavernier[49] (who shall be our cicerone) reached the Maidan at dawn on the morning of 3 July 1667, and was conducted to an excellent seat that had been reserved for him on one of the balconies near the Ali Qapu. Not long after, the Shah (Sulaiman II) appeared with some of his courtiers on the terrace of the Ali Qapu, where a throne had been placed in readiness. There then followed five hours of parades, dancing, and mock battles which later in the day degenerated into real ones: for the city was swarming with peasants—wild-looking men with plumes in their turbans and big clubs in their hands, who had come up from the country for a spree. A number of people were always killed before the day was out; but it was a good time to die, for a direct passage to paradise was guaranteed to all who lost their lives during the festival.

One of the features of the parade was a procession of pikemen, each with the head of an Özbeg on the top of his pike. Then three hundred Turkish prisoners were led in, to plead for mercy and receive the royal pardon. Troupes of boy dancers performed very gracefully, beating time with little sticks. Next came a number of waggons, elegantly decorated with gold and silver arabesques, each bearing a coffin covered with satin. Every waggon was accompanied by its bodyguard, armed with clubs 'almost as big as levers' for use later on. As the waggons approached the royal box, the richly caparisoned horses that drew them broke into a gallop.

> Then all the company fell a running and dancing about with the bier. Besides that, everyone flung up his short cassock, his girdle, and bonnet, put their fingers in their mouths, to whistle as loud as they could. While the naked people, with their flint-stones in their hands, ran knocking their stones together, crying out, *Hussein Hocen, Hocen Hussein*, till they foam at the mouth again; not omitting to writhe their bodies, and to make all the scurvy faces as before described....

42. Fragment of tile mosaic from the Rasiazeh Madraseh at Isfahan. It probably dates from the sixteenth century. *Victoria and Albert Museum, London.*

43

At this point a riot broke out. The major-domo, with great presence of mind, quickly summoned five elephants which created a diversion by performing circus tricks. When order had been restored, a *mulla* in the royal box preached a half-hour sermon and the Shah withdrew.

But for the crowds the day's fun was only beginning: far into the night the rival waggon-teams paraded the streets, waging pitched battles whenever they chanced to meet. These combats were largely the result of Abbas the Great's rash creation, in Isfahan and elsewhere in Persia, of two rival bands—the Ni'mat Allahi and the Haidari, also known as the Palank and Falank. Though their members were forbidden the use of military weapons, they managed to do a wonderful amount of damage to one another with sticks and stones. Abbas had always encouraged these street fights, which amused him greatly.

Such was the major festival of the year; but there were many others also. The solar year opened on 21 March with *Nauruz* (New Year's Day) which the Persians celebrate much as the French do, with gifts and the exchange of visits, with the wearing of new clothes and with feasting. The Festival of Roses was a time of dancing and singing, of coffee-drinking and picnicking in the country. At this season the ganymede boys issued at night from their coffee-houses, accompanied by men with torches, and scattered roses upon the passers-by in return for money. On the twenty-first day of *Ramadan* came the Feast of Ali, which followed much the same pattern as the Festival of Husain and also ended in brawls and broken skulls.

THE WATER FESTIVAL

For all these festivals the Maidan was naturally the focal point. There was also, however, the great Water Festival—the *Ab Pashan*, or ' Aspersion '—which was held on the banks of the Zayandeh-rud near the Thirty-three-arch bridge. It took place at irregular intervals, but normally in the early summer before the river had begun to run dry. Della Valle, who was present at the *Ab Pashan* in 1619, has left a full account of it. The Shah was always present; and on this occasion he was accompanied by several ambassadors, including the Spaniard Don Garcia da Figueroa, who happened to be in Isfahan at the time.

The *Ab Pashan* was, it seems, a rough-and-tumble water-fight fraught with considerable danger for the participants. The whole male population of the town, dressed in short and shabby Mazandaran tunics and wearing their oldest caps, assembled early in the morning by the water's edge carrying large brass bowls.

> On a signal from the Shah they begin hurling water at one another, laughing, leaping about and shouting—a very gay spectacle. In doing this they get so excited that in the end they completely lose their heads. Either in anger, or for the mere fun of it, they begin to play the fool and push one another into the river with such violence that no festival ever passes without one or two people being drowned.[50]

Don Garcia was sixty-eight years of age, ' white-haired, but still very active '. He was, however, beginning to find the pace of life at the Persian court extremely exhausting. Though a teetotaller, he was constantly forced to drink wine; and the food disagreed with him. He disliked the formal dress which he was obliged to wear even in the hottest weather. Sitting cross-legged on the ground gave him cramp. He hated the noise and the dust and the heat and the late hours. Moreover his mission was a delicate one, for he had been sent to Persia to urge the Shah to respect Portuguese possessions in the Persian Gulf. He was a reluctant observer of what, to a hidalgo, must have seemed sheer horseplay.

Abbas always enjoyed pulling Don Garcia's leg. As they sat carousing, the conversation turned to the subject of dancing girls. Now it had caused some surprise

43. Mural decoration (seventeenth century). *Victoria and Albert Museum, London.*

97

at court, and not a little amusement, that the Spaniard had shown no inclination to avail himself of the services of the girls who, in the ordinary course of hospitality, had been put at his disposal. ' It's no use your pretending to be virtuous ', said Abbas rudely. ' The plain fact is that you are too old for it '.

The courtiers laughed; but Don Garcia was not amused. He replied curtly that the women offered him were miserable wenches who would not have disturbed the composure of even a young man. It would be a different matter if the Shah were to send him one or two of the beauties whom he kept hidden away in his harem. Abbas did not join in the laughter that greeted this sally; he rose and, snatching the turban from the head of one of his ministers, to serve him for a pillow, he withdrew to take a short nap.

Meanwhile the water-party was getting quite out of hand. Men were hitting one another on the head with their brass bowls, and throwing one another into the stream. Abbas, roused at last from his sleep, came back to put a stop to the fun, and the Isfahanis staggered off to the town to bandage up their wounds. It had been a successful day: no less than five people had been drowned.

THE AMBASSADORS

These festivals deserve detailed description because they afford us a picture, not only of the way of life of the people, but also of the Shahs and their courtiers. So too do the experiences of the many ambassadors and envoys who at one time or another came to Persia.

In the autumn of 1618, a number of foreign ambassadors arrived at the court of Abbas the Great, amongst them two Russians—Kinas Ivan Votorinsky and Ivan Ivanovich. Abbas was at the time in Qazvin, where he entertained his guests with the customary illuminations and animal fights in the Maidan. Pietro Della Valle was also there, and he describes with some relish the barbaric appearance of the Russians:

> The dress of these Russians seems to me to be coarse and ugly. It reaches down to the ankles, is very broad throughout and pleated everywhere in the most haphazard manner. The waist is bound by an ugly belt, and a large hood—much fuller than those worn nowadays by Roman Senators—reaches half way down the back. They wear their hair as long as we do, and on their heads a small pointed cap lined with fur. The Ambassadors and their secretary alone wear these caps very high and lined with sable. The fur is wound so far up the cap that the top is invisible; I never saw anything so odd in my life. The Ambassadors and their secretary were dressed alike, in red silk with a mass of pearls in their caps as was their custom. The others were mostly in purple cloth, the minor officials in white and a few others in colours. They were all very pale-skinned, but with faces red from heavy drinking, fair-haired, and with long beards. They lived dirtily, and I have been told that they do not think twice about wiping their greasy fingers on their coats, even when they are of brocade. They are by nature proud and uncouth, faithless, deceivers it is said, and, above all, irreconcilable enemies of the Church of Rome.

The Russians brought gifts of furs, tusks, great lanterns with talc windows, and a large consignment of vodka of various qualities. Abbas pretended to be affronted by the vodka, suggesting that his guests seemed to be in greater need of it than he was; none the less, he kept the choicest bottles before returning the rest.

Votorinsky, already a sick man, died at Qazvin soon after, but his colleague made his way in the spring to Isfahan, where Abbas proposed to entertain the ambassadors more brilliantly than he had been able to do in Qazvin. Della Valle, on the spot as always, has described the events that followed. The English resident and the Spanish ambassador were already in Isfahan when Abbas arrived, but the three other ambassadors were stationed at Daulatabad, about seven miles from the capital. The Englishman was a simple fellow who did not stand on his dignity. The Spaniard, Don Garcia, on the other hand, had become truculent and moody, always ready to take offence, and he failed to join his colleagues for the **state** entry into the city. Truth to tell, the unwonted dissipation and the late hours, the Persian cuisine that turned his stomach, the wine that—though a teetotaller—he was often obliged to drink, the noise, the heat and the dust, the ridiculously unseasonable fancy-dress that he had to wear, and a hundred other petty irritations, had combined to reduce him at last to a pitiable state.

Della Valle went out to Daulatabad to take part in the magnificent progress of the ambassadors and their suites. The Indian ambassador was attended with peculiar pomp. Palanquins (which Della Valle considered a lazy and effeminate method of transport) and elephants bearing drums so large that each beast could only carry one pair, were novelties that did not fail to excite the Italian's curiosity. Besides the drums, which were played incessantly by Indians and made an ear-splitting din, he noticed ' a large number of trumpets of prodigious size, shaped like those which our artists give to Fame '.

The way from Daulatabad was closely lined on both sides by 60,000 infantry-men—not regulars, but artisans and shopkeepers who had been pressed into service to swell the majesty of the occasion; they wore the gayest clothes, with great plumes in their hats. Court officials riding splendidly caparisoned horses, Jews chanting and praying and holding lighted candles, Christians from Julfa, squadrons of cavalry, men and women from Isfahan and the surrounding country, and twenty-five of Isfahan's most seductive courtesans, unveiled and on horseback, all joined, formally or informally, in the wild concourse that thronged the seven-mile route, so that a whole day was passed in processions, in singing and in dancing.

Della Valle noticed with amusement the extraordinary effect of music on the Persians, for ' even the soldiers who had to keep their ranks and hold their arquebuses could not contain themselves, but with endless gesticulations, with legs quivering and buttocks wriggling, gave, without ever moving from their places, a thousand signs of the terpsichorean frenzy that possessed them '.

The ambassadors were received at the Palace gates by a troupe of young boys, magnificently dressed, who proffered them iced drinks. Della Valle, after paying his respects to Abbas, went home to wash and rest, while the Indian, whose pomp and fine presents had secured him privileged treatment, remained to dine privately with the Shah. The Spaniard, indignant at the favours showered upon what he termed ' a mere merchant ', sulked in his house, but was later prevailed upon to come to the Palace for the reception given by Abbas.

Meanwhile not only the 60,000 infantrymen but the entire population of the surrounding villages surged into Isfahan. Soon the streets were so densely packed that no one could move; every window, every balcony, every roof-top was filled to saturation point. Then, as the Eastern night descended swiftly upon the expectant city, the order was given for torches and lanterns to be lit.

For, as at Qazvin, a series of night festivals was to form the principal ingredient of the fare provided to amuse the foreigners. The Maidan and a large part of the town, including the Mint and a section of the Bazaar, had been shut off from the rest of the city. Every male had been excluded from this area so that the Shah's harem might enjoy the display, and Della Valle tells us that even ' a number of repulsive old hags, whose hideous appearance might turn the stomachs of the King and his ladies ', were to be removed from the enclosure on certain evenings. The presence of the better-looking women of the town had, however, not merely been encouraged but actually commanded; these flocked to the gates of the enclosure, where more than 2000 of them were passed by the eunuchs on guard as comely enough to enter.

Abbas, his two sons and his guests, now issued from the Palace and made their way, not without difficulty, across the Maidan to the coffee-houses at the northern end of the square.

They were described at length by Della Valle:

> These enormous rooms, white-walled and clean, are open on all sides, and since they lead into one another they seem to be one vast building. They were a blaze of light, not with formally hung lanterns as elsewhere, but with myriads of lamps suspended high up in the domes and giving the impression of a starry sky. And since each room had its pool under the dome, the ground seemed as star-spangled as the ceilings.

While refreshments were being served, a number of the pretty, effeminately dressed boys attached to the establishment came forward to give a display of dancing. The Spanish ambassador was considerably shocked by the lascivious posturing of a Circassian and a Persian who performed a competition dance. The Persian lad's father, a tight-rope dancer from Shiraz, caused a good deal of amusement by the gestures and grimaces with which he urged on his son to victory. To the general discomfort, the Indian ambassador puffed away at his long gold pipe with a bowl the size of a hen's egg.

Then the Shah and his guests set out to view the town. First the Mint was visited, with its glowing furnaces and great ingots of gold and silver. Next they passed to the shops:

> Here and there the King stopped to chat or take a cup of wine, first in the shop of Mek Beg, chief of the Tabriz merchants, who kept the richest store in Isfahan, then in that of our Venetian Alessandro Scudendoli, the second finest, which was full of pictures, mirrors and other Italian curios. The King treated Scudendoli with great cordiality and showed the Indian Ambassador the paintings (which were mostly portraits of princes, of the kind that sell for a crown apiece in the Piazza Navona in Rome but which here fetch ten sequins and are considered cheap at the price), inviting him to pick out whatever he liked and promising to pay for them himself. But the Indian scornfully refused.

At another shop Abbas found a bottle of wine particularly to his taste and carried it off with him.

> All this time the King was chatting with the Ambassadors, laughing and cracking jokes (for you know his gay though whimsical sense of humour), and especially with the Spaniard and the Indian whom he always favoured above the others. The Spanish Ambassador, a serious-minded man who sets store by solemnity, he embraced and addressed as *Babà* (that is, ' grandfather ') and the like, all in the most respectful way. But the Indian Ambassador, who like all his countrymen is hearty and fond of a joke, he treated more familiarly, continually giving him great digs in the back which, since he is stout and—as is the local custom—only dressed in a single garment of very fine linen, must undoubtedly have hurt him a great deal. Sometimes he would come quite close to him as if to whisper something, and then seize him by both ears and pull hard; sometimes he roared with laughter and called him *Pir ghidi*, that is ' old cuckold ' (though for that matter he himself is no chicken). In short, he behaved in a way which, though it seemed to be merely free and easy, was actually very insulting. Possibly the King did this to pay him back for his insolence and for the contempt that he always shows for everything of His Majesty's.
> Then the Russians, who are a barbarous and rude people, came up behind us and butted. They are so big and strong, and pushed so hard, that we had the greatest difficulty in preventing the King, who is rather small, from being swept off his feet. The Turkish Ambassador too, who though he had a very high opinion of himself was not a favourite, also came in for insults from the crowd. As he was leaving the Mint, where the Russians were pressing hard, a group of courtiers (probably thinking it would amuse the King) pushed and jostled him so badly that his suite were unable to save him from being knocked over, and there were roars of laughter when his turban came off. He was as angry as he was surprised, and swore at all this unseemly behaviour which was so foreign to his nature and to that of his countrymen. I, in all innocence, got involved in the affray, for being pushed from behind I was obliged to trample on him to avoid falling—a happy omen, perhaps....

After another collation at the coffee-house, during which the Shah ' refused to sit, but wandered up and down looking more like the manager of the establishment than a King ', the Spanish ambassador—utterly worn out and already half asleep—withdrew with his suite. Della Valle, to avoid remaining at table where the conversation was not to his liking, soon followed his lead. Then Abbas himself slipped silently away. But his remaining guests, quite undisturbed by the absence of their host, drank on until dawn broke.

44. Dancing girl.
A miniature of the Isfahan school,
c. 1590. *Treasury,
Topkapi Palace Museum, Istanbul.*

Christian residents

BESIDES THE MANY travellers and diplomats who visited Isfahan in the seventeenth century, there was also a hard core of resident Christians. These comprised a large Armenian community, a number of Roman Catholic missionaries, and the 'Factors' of the Trading Companies established by the English, French and Dutch.

JULFA—THE ARMENIAN COLONY

Early in the seventeenth century—probably in the autumn of the year 1603—Abbas the Great forcibly transplanted the entire population of several thousand families from the Armenian town of Julfa, in Azerbaijan, to his new capital. One contemporary authority says that their reluctance to migrate was overcome when the Shah sent troops to cut off their water supply. The Julfans were given land on the south bank of the Zayandeh-rud, a little upstream from Isfahan; they were allowed to build churches and practise their Christian rites, and to appoint a *kalantar*, or mayor, of their own nationality. Abbas loaned them money without interest, so that they could establish themselves and open up trade.

Two reasons have been suggested for this remarkable experiment. It was said that Abbas wanted to deprive the Turks of one of their chief marts for provisions. It was also said that he imported these thrifty and hard-working Armenians to be an object lesson to his own subjects and a stimulus to international trade. Very probably the latter factor weighed more heavily with the Shah.

The Christian suburb flourished. Its population soon reached at least 30,000—some say double this number—and for nearly a century the town fulfilled its object of setting an example of industry to the lazy and happy-go-lucky Isfahanis. But already by Chardin's time there were signs that its days of prosperity were numbered. Taxes were increased, sympathy was withdrawn. Shah Sulaiman began a mild persecution which, under his inflexibly orthodox successor Shah Sultan Husain, became a calculated campaign of violence. Goods were confiscated, privileges taken away. A law was promulgated that if a Persian killed an Armenian he need only pay one load of corn to the family of the dead man. Any Armenian who turned Muslim inherited all the effects of any relation, however distant, on his death.

But under Abbas the Great the city throve. Soon there was a Cathedral and a dozen other churches, a monastery, and a nunnery for 'thirty impoverished, ugly and misshapen widows and girls'. The Armenians became rich; their wives dressed in 'striped satins purfled with gold'; and their houses were luxuriously furnished. Chardin visited one of the finest—it was down by the river and little less than a palace, he thought—at which Abbas II and Safi were often guests. When Herbert dined one evening with an Armenian 'Prince', Shiraz wine flowed uninterruptedly from golden flagons into golden bowls, and there was delicious food which included roast pork; but the house was 'furnished with such beastly pictures, such ugly postures as indeed are not fit to be remembered'.[51] These were the work of a certain Minas, who studied with a European artist in Aleppo and then returned to

45. Courtyard of the College of the Mother of the Shah (early eighteenth century).

Persia where he found employment decorating the houses of wealthy Julfans. Erotic paintings were especially common in Islamic countries in the *hammams*, where, according to a fourteenth-century physician, they helped to repair the vigour lost through the enervating pleasures of bathing.

The Cathedral Church of All Saviour's (also known as the ' Vank ') was begun in 1606, but virtually rebuilt when it was considerably enlarged fifty years later. It is a simple contruction, now faced externally with relatively modern brick to preserve it, and crowned with a dome in the Persian manner. Internally however there are certain concessions—for example, an apse and a raised chancel—to Western usage. In the courtyard are a large free-standing belfry and a number of graves of Protestant Christians as well as of Armenians. A charming little museum contains manuscripts and costumes, together with various historical objects and minor *objets d'art*.

After the brightness of the Persian mosques, the interior of the Cathedral strikes the visitor as somewhat heavy and confused. Above a wainscot of splendid tiles and a wonderful painted border of flowers, the walls are covered with darkened Italianate paintings, many of which represent scenes of torture more calculated to turn the stomach that to uplift the spirit; and over the entrance is a Last Judgment, so placed as to give a parting prod at the consciences of the worshippers. These works of art were the gift of an Armenian merchant named Avadich who had travelled in Italy. Avadich had some difficulty, it seems, in persuading his co-religionists to accept them; and needless to say they shocked the Muslims. Perhaps the most attractive feature of the interior is the delicately painted blue and gold ceiling of the dome, exquisite as the border of a Safavid illuminated manuscript. The liturgy in this and the other Armenian churches in Julfa is conducted in the ancient Armenian tongue.

About a mile from Julfa is the Armenian Cemetery. The spot is arid and desolate; but it is impossible not to be moved by the sight of the ' great blocks or slabs of stone, chiselled and sculptured,'[52] which mark the last resting-places, not only of innumerable Armenians who have died in Julfa during the last 350 years, but of many Europeans also. Here lie Frenchmen, Englishmen, Dutchmen, Russians and others who came to Isfahan to trade or to satisfy their curiosity. Best known of all is the grave of Rudolph Stadler (or Sadler), a Swiss watchmaker who for a time enjoyed the favour of Shah Safi, but who was ultimately put to death at his command. Olearius and Tavernier both give a full account of Stadler's brilliant career, which was cut short when he was still only twenty-eight.

Tavernier made the acquaintance of Stadler in Constantinople, where he was in the service of the Sultan. Greatly impressed by his skill, the Frenchman took the young watchmaker with him to Isfahan and helped to set him up in business. A little striking watch that Stadler made, no bigger than a half-crown, was purchased by some English merchants for presentation to Imam Quli Khan, the popular and kindly old Governor of Shiraz, who in turn gave it to the Shah. Safi was delighted with it and wore it always on a gold chain under his clothing; he had never seen so small a striking watch before. Then one day he overwound it and broke the mainspring. Stadler was sent for and quickly put it right; but thereafter the Shah thought it best for the watchmaker to call every morning at the Palace to wind it up for him.

The Shah took a great fancy to Stadler, and paid him handsomely for this trivial task. Each morning the young Swiss was greeted with a glass of wine, and for a while the two men would gossip together. Again and again Safi begged him to turn Muslim, promising him promotion and wealth; but Stadler was not to be persuaded.

Ambassadors and merchants who came to Isfahan soon saw that great advantage was to be gained from cultivating a man who had the ear of the Shah. In particular, two ambassadors from the Duke of Holstein, who were in Isfahan in 1637, made much fuss of the Swiss watchmaker and often invited him to parties at their house. One night, after he had ' tarried late upon the debauch with them ', Stadler returned home to find a Persian, the brother of one of the royal porters, skulking in his courtyard. Now Stadler had a young Nestorian mistress; when the Persian guiltily jumped over the wall and made his escape through the garden, the object of his visit was not hard to guess. Stadler kept watch, and a few days later succeeded in catching the man red-handed. With the help of his servants Stadler tied the Persian to a tree in the courtyard and want to bed; the servants, however, hung about

Fig. 14. Julfa: The Armenian Cathedral (from *La Perse*, by Mme Dieulafoy, 1887).

tormenting their victim. Finally one of them rashly came within range of the Persian who, his legs being free, gave him so savage a kick in the groin that it killed him. Woken by the noise, Stadler came out and, seizing his pistol, shot the Persian dead.

At the morning ceremony of watch-winding, the Shah asked Stadler for the latest news. After hearing the whole story he observed that Stadler had acted rightly. But unfortunately the Swiss had made a powerful enemy at court—the *Itimad al-Daula* (Prime Minister)—who succeeded in convincing Safi that Stadler had misrepresented the facts and that this was the moment to compel him to turn Muslim or suffer death. Though offered a large sum of money and a wife (together with all her jewels) from the royal harem, Stadler would not budge; orders were therefore given for him to be handed over to the porter and his kin. The ambassadors attempted to obtain an audience with Safi, but were outmanoeuvred by the wily Minister. The Fathers were chiefly concerned with trying to effect a last-minute conversion from the heresies of the Reformed Church to the True Faith; but to Stadler, Rome was almost as distasteful as Islam.

The execution took place at the end of October, 1637, in the Maidan, all the Franks and the Armenian clergy being obliged to attend. Stadler, a *palenk* (triangular wooden halter) round his neck, was led into the Maidan, where the porter and his relations awaited him. The porter gave the first blow; but his sword glanced off one of the sides of the *palenk* and seriously wounded one of his brothers in the leg. Another brother missed altogether. Then the third struck and felled Stadler to the ground, though he was obliged to strike three more times to kill him.

By Safi's order, Stadler's blood was collected in a vessel and his body buried beneath a twelve-foot tomb, erected by subscription among the Franks and inscribed with the simple legend:

CY GIT RODOLFE

The Armenians spread a rumour that angels had descended to guard the tomb on the night following the burial, and soon there were reports of miraculous cures of sick persons who prayed there and then carried away a piece of the stone. This made the upkeep of the grave a very heavy expense. As for the Shah—his watch went wrong a few days after Stadler's death, and his apprentice was unable to mend it. This misfortune came near to costing the Prime Minister his life, Safi blaming him for the loss of the best craftsman in Isfahan. There was, however, a silver lining to the cloud of Stadler's death: during the remaining years of his reign, Safi, though often much provoked, allowed no more Franks to be executed.

From this long digression we return to the other graves in the Julfa cemetery, among which Browne observed one or two English tombstones. There are also several graves of members of the de l'Estoile family, who came from Lyon to Isfahan in the eighteenth century. Another is that of Jacob Rousseau, a Genevan clock-maker and great-uncle of the famous Jean-Jacques, who died in Isfahan in 1753, having lived there for forty-eight years and survived the siege of the city by the Afghans.

THE ROMAN CATHOLIC MISSIONS

Not long after his accession, Abbas the Great had entered into correspondence with the newly elected Pope, Clement VIII. Negotiations had also been opened between the Shah and Philip III of Spain and Portugal. These led to the arrival of Italian Carmelite and Portuguese Augustinian missionaries in Isfahan at the beginning of the seventeenth century.

By this time there were already many Christian establishments in the Orient. The Franciscans had been ' Guardians of the Holy Sepulchre ' since 1496, and were also to be found in many parts of the Near East; they claim to have had a church in Pekin in 1299, and were certainly in India by 1534. During the sixteenth century the Dominicans and the Jesuits had established themselves all over the Far East, and the Augustinians in Hormuz, the Philippines and Goa. The Capuchins, and the newly-founded Discalced Carmelites, had not yet undertaken missionary work in the East.

Several Portuguese Augustinians, among them Father Antonio da Gouvea, were the first Christian missionaries to settle in the new Persian capital; they probably arrived there in the year 1603. Abbas had questions to regulate with the Portuguese of Goa and Hormuz; he also hoped to trade with Portugal in Persian silks, and to find in Philip III an ally against the Turks: he therefore greeted the missionaries cordially. Father Antonio relates that the Shah was ' very affectionate ' with him, ' having kissed me on the neck more than 10 times, embraced me an infinite number, many times he gave me to drink with his own hand, and paid me many other politenesses '. This display of affection was due to the fact that Philip had

46. Zinc flask inlaid with gold and semi-precious stones, dating from the Safavid period. *Treasury, Topkapi Palace Museum, Istanbul.*

recently promised to send gunners, engineers and artillery to the Shah if he allowed the Gospel to be preached in his realm.

Another Augustinian, Father Paul Simon of Jesus Mary, believed that Abbas was ready to submit to baptism; but the Shah seemed to be always too busy to come to a definite decision. He would, he said, discuss the matter more fully 'when he had the opportunity'. However, he kept the Augustinians, for the time being, 'almost always near him'. He allowed them to choose a house, gave them 2000 *scudi* a year for their keep, and invited them to banquets at which they were invariably placed beside him. He even conducted one of them into his harem, which his own son might not enter, and made his women entertain the guest by dancing. He promised to construct a church with bells in every town captured from the Turks, and to permit the Gospel to be preached, if Philip sent artillery and engineers. (Philip had, of course, no more intention of sending guns which could be used against him in Hormuz, than had Abbas of submitting to baptism.)

Abbas also went to the Augustinian church and with his own hands decked the altar. He asked for a fragment of the wood of the True Cross, and it was immediately produced and given to him.

> When he drank, and in public, he used to do so with an old Father of the Augustinians, a great servant of God and much liked by the King, he would make for him the sign of the Cross over the drinking-glass; and by many other signs he showed himself well disposed towards our Holy Faith.[54]

A letter survives, written by Abbas to Pope Clement VIII, probably in the year 1603, and couched in splendid oriental hyperbole:

> Lord Pope of Rome,
> [The preamble apostrophizes the Sovereign Pontiff in untranslatable epithets as the supreme master of all professing the Christian Faith.]
> ... After the establishing of the basis of amity and love, and expressing the utmost sincerity and unity, it is submitted to Your sunlike notice and moonlike mind that at this auspicious season the cordial communication, which You had dispatched by those eloquent envoys, namely that most distinguished of Christian literati, the priest Francisco Costa, and that respected gentleman, Diego Miranda, arrived at a most fortunate juncture ...

The story of these two Portuguese rogues, Don Diego de Miranda and Father Francisco da Costa S. J., is most curious. They had reached Rome from the East Indies, where they were resident, by way of Persia. In Rome they obtained an audience with the Pope, to whom they reported that the Shah was about to send emissaries to the Vatican; it would be wise, they said, for the Pope to anticipate this by an embassy to Abbas. Pope Clement believed their story, which may or may not have been true, and granted them 4,000 *scudi* to go as his representatives to Persia.

The envoys quarrelled even before they left Venice, committed follies in Poland and 'base acts' in Moscow where they imposed upon the credulity of the Grand Duke. In Astrakhan, where they spent the winter, Father Francisco stole Don Diego's clothes and belongings, leaving him nearly naked. On reaching Persia, Don Diego succeeded in having Father Francisco put in chains, and with money that he stole from a Venetian trader...

> ... set up an establishment, engaging some thirty servants, and he had liveries made and silverware, he bought richly adorned tents, velvet chairs, carpets, a canopy under which he was wont to sit, horses and other articles for becoming pomp and show. He kept a splendid table. Besides pages and grooms, when he went out he took two men, who each of them bore a silver mace, and another who bore in front of him a standard with His Holiness' arms. With this ceremony he went off to the King...
> When Don Diego came to the King, he seated himself at the Shah's side and began to speak of various matters. The King asked him whether he brought letters from His Holiness. He an-

47. Talar of the Chihil Sutun (seventeenth century).

swered 'Yes', and took out the Brief from his [breeches] pocket, and told the Shah to stand up to receive it. The Shah replied, 'If you had brought it with the respect due, and not from behind, not only would I have got up, but I would have gone out to receive it.'

Whenever he was on horseback with the King he would ride at Abbas's side, and in front of him had borne the standard of His Holiness. He did other things, for which the King, who is discerning and well-informed of the ways things are done over here, used to call him 'the Fool'. The Shah gave him 2,000 *scudi* for his needs and a fine horse as well as other things...

But Don Diego's theft from the Venetian trader now caught up with him, and he was obliged to restore the stolen money and leave the country. Meanwhile Father

Fig. 15. Bazaar at Julfa (from *La Perse*, by Mme Dieulafoy, 1887).

Francisco had made his escape and, reaching Isfahan, was presented by the Augustinians to Abbas who, in spite of his experience with Don Diego, treated him at first with great generosity and kindness.

Father Francisco was always about the Shah. Once, when the Father was seated, the very Shah himself on his knees [55] gave him to drink, in order to show the respect he had for the Pope. He caused Father Francisco's portrait to be painted, as the garb of a prelate with rochet ... took his fancy. But in the end Father Francisco lost the Shah's favour through certain indiscretions.' [56]

These included the theft of money, the abduction of an Armenian boy, and much else besides. Don Diego and Father Francisco must have been cunning rogues to have successfully imposed upon both the Pope and the Shah for so long.

Perhaps it was because of the unfortunate impression created by the first Jesuit in Isfahan, that the Society of Jesus did not establish itself in Julfa until 1653. The Jesuits were never there in strength, though their House did in fact continue until, in 1757, the position of all Christian missionaries became intolerable.

In 1604, the Pope decided to send several Carmelite Fathers to Isfahan.

The difficulties and disasters of the journey, by way of Russia, which because of illness and incessant setbacks took more than three years, has been described by their leader, Father Paul Simon.[57] The Fathers reached Isfahan on 2 December 1607, but it was not until a month later—for Father Paul Simon had arrived with a high fever—that they were received in audience by Abbas.

They found the Shah in his stables, selecting horses for the war; he was 'seated on a mound, on a cheap carpet, and dressed in black cloth because it was ' Lent ' (i. e. Ramadan). After the usual compliments had been exchanged, and in spite of the presence of two Turkish emissaries, the Turkish situation was discussed; then the Fathers' gifts were produced and presented to the Shah. Abbas was particularly pleased with a crucifix in which the figure of Christ was of gold on a cross of Bohemian crystal.

An illuminated manuscript of the Old Testament was now opened and examined. It is not stated whether the Carmelites had brought this with them, but there is no doubt that it was what is now known as the Pierpont Morgan *Book of Old Testament Illustrations*, a superb volume of Parisian workmanship, dating from the middle of the thirteenth century.[58] ' The King opened the book by chance at the page where the combat between the good angels and the bad is related. When he saw the dragon vanquished and prostrate at the feet of St Michael, who was brandishing his sword and threatening the Devil, the King inquired: " Who is that who is vanquished at the feet of the angel? " Father Paul replied: " That is the fallen angel whom we call the Devil ". " No ", said the Shah, laughing heartily; " That is the Turk (i. e. the Sultan) ". As he said it, he continued to laugh, glancing over his shoulder at the Turkish Pashas, for he never lost an opportunity to mock at them. He charged a *mulla* to write on each page of this book of miniatures in the Persian language what they represented; and, so that they might do it the more correctly, to consult the Carmelites '.

The Shah asked the Fathers to excuse him for not inviting them to stay to supper, since it was Ramadan and he was observing the fast. He had no religious scruples, however, about accepting a small barrel of vodka which the Fathers had brought with them from Russia, and ' could not find words to thank them for so acceptable a gift '. Father Simon observed—and perhaps with some satisfaction, for inevitably there was some rivalry between the two religious Orders—that the Shah did not address a single word to the Augustinians.

Two days later came a second audience, held in the *talar* of the Ali Qapu where Abbas had invited his guests to watch a display of bull- and ram-fighting. Father Simon seized the opportunity to tell the Shah that the Pope was urging Christendom to unite and attack the Turks by sea; this news so delighted Abbas that he paid no further attention to the combats in the Maidan.

After one of their audiences with Abbas, the Shah commanded the Carmelites to pray for him ' till further notice '. It clearly amused him to keep them under the impression that he might at any moment be converted to Christianity. Father Simon long continued in hope; but within a year of their arrival, Father John Thaddeus had guessed the truth. He wrote to Rome:

> As to the character of this King, he is at heart a Muhammadan, and all he has done in the past has been feigned. Now that he has won so many victories over the Turks, he does not care a jot for all the Christian princes and publicly mocks at them because they do not make war on the Turks, or that when they do so they are defeated. You should not imagine that he will give us a church, or permission to make Christians of his subjects; on the contrary, he is always trying, whenever he can, to get Armenian Christians, Franks, and those of any other race, to become Muslims ...

Father John continued:

> Till now there has been small success in conversions [to Roman Catholicism], for the Muslims are as already described, and the Armenians, so the Augustinian Fathers say, take no account of the Pope unless it be to get money or temporal benefit ... It appears to us that great results could

be gained in this country if there were a College for Armenian, Georgian, Circassian and Persian boys, who might be purchased out of the many offered for sale. If we could bring them up among us and teach them our habits and standards of conduct, we could send them to Italy when they were older and they could be used as interpreters. The King of Persia would not interfere with such work; we do not doubt this, because it is the custom here that a slave must take the religion of his master. Many souls would thus be released from the bonds of Satan, since many of them would become our brethren and others would follow them.

The Carmelites, on their arrival in Isfahan, were conducted to a house ' prepared inside the city ', but it was ' not very good ' and they changed lodging several times before they were finally established, in June 1609, in the building which they were to occupy continuously for nearly 150 years.

In spite of topographical details given by Father John Thaddeus, and of the general view of Isfahan reproduced in Olearius's *Travels* in which the various convents are marked, it is impossible today to identify the actual site of the Carmelite Convent. The house stood to the west of the Maidan, and was one of the many ' palaces ' which Abbas had appropriated in Isfahan; the Carmelites never obtained the freehold, and this was often to be the cause of anxiety to them. Father John describes it as being situated ' in a very wide level open space ', and being ' like an island in the midst of a very large garden '. There was a constant supply of running water for irrigation, in a channel four spans wide, and also a well with good drinking water.

The house itself, when they took it over, looked more like ' a stable for camels ' than a palace, but by degrees the Fathers succeeded in altering it to suit their needs. Their first concern was the transformation of the ' hall ' into a chapel, making use of a number of carpets which they found in the building, and Mass was said there for the first time on St John's Day (24 June), 1609. Then came cells, a refectory, a kitchen, and other domestic offices. By 1616, 25,000 vines had been planted in the grounds. Over the entrance—perhaps the entrance to the estate rather than of the house itself—was inscribed, " The House of God and Jesus (and) Mary ", written in large gilt letters, Latin above and Persian below, so that Muslims passing in the street and reading the names of Jesus and Mary, often make signs of respect towards it '.[59]

In the 1630s the chapel was replaced by a proper church with ' four side-chapels besides the high altar, and on the façade there is a great cross, which can be seen from afar. There are two fair-sized bells, which are rung day and night at the hours observed by the Rule of the Order—a privilege rarely conceded in Muhammadan countries ...'

The rise and fall of the Carmelite mission can be gauged from the various reports mentioning the number of religious in residence. In 1621 there were ' fifteen in the house to feed, including servants and boys '. In 1636 there were seven religious, and by 1650 nine religious and another three about to arrive from Europe. Then numbers began to fall off. In 1692 there were four Fathers and a Lay Brother in Isfahan itself, and five Fathers in Julfa; but ten years later only two missionaries remained in the city.

Their business is to read the Gospel over sick infidels, men, women and children, who daily come in large numbers to beg this favour wherefore, when the Fathers perceive some infallible and near peril of death, they baptise the children. Indeed during the past sixteen years, as I have seen in the register, they have baptised more than 7,000, all dead—none baptised remained alive ...[60]

On the eve of the Afghan invasion, the Vicar Provincial, Father Faustin of St Charles, after praising the convents of the Augustinians and Capuchins, could still write:

48. Fountain in the grounds of the Chihil Sutun.

49

Our house is, however, the largest and now the most beautiful and commodious of all, as I have repaired and rearranged it in a way that those who saw it previously would now no longer recognize it. And this without having spent even a penny of our subsidy, but with money obtained from the sale of some specimens of clocks and other things unnecessary for this house ... Believe me, Reverend Father, that in Europe we have many Convents not the half of this, and it seems to me a great glory for the Lord to have it—a house so fine, and a church where our Observance is followed ...[61]

THE FACTORS

Mention has already been made of the activities of the English and Dutch East India Companies in Persia.

A Surat merchant named Richard Steele first proposed that the English Company might open up trade with Persia. In 1614, while travelling through the country on his way to India, he noticed what little personal protection the Persians had against the extreme cold of their winters. Now the Company had been having some difficulty in disposing of all its stocks of cloth in India; Steele therefore, on reaching Surat, suggested this new market for its surplus stores.

Sir Thomas Roe, English ambassador to the Mughal court, at first opposed the scheme, but Steele overcame his objections. In 1617, after the ground had been carefully prepared by Steele and one of his colleagues, factories were opened in Isfahan and Shiraz, and two years later at the port of Jask. Shah Abbas offered the most favourable terms: trade was to be unrestricted throughout the country and factors allowed free exercise of their religion; an English ambassador might reside permanently in Isfahan, and any Englishman who became involved in a criminal case was to be under his jurisdiction. The Shah further promised to supply the Company annually with between 1000 and 3000 bales of silk for duty-free shipment from Jask.

Abbas of course hoped for benefits from these concessions, and five years later the Company felt itself obliged—though with much reluctance—to allow its ships to help in the expulsion of the Portuguese from Hormuz and Qishm; this resulted, for the English, in the permanent enmity of the Portuguese, but also in further trade concessions at 'Gombroon' (Bandar Abbas), which Abbas now designed to replace Jask as his principal port.

The Dutch East India Company had been founded in 1602, two years after the English Company; it was a truly national institution and far more richly subsidized than the English. Soon after the English factory had been moved from Jask to Gombroon, the Dutch set up a larger factory nearby. Relations were at this time very strained between England and Holland, yet their common fear of the combined might of Spain and Portugal drew them together in self-defence.

Though the English had had a start of six years, the Dutch, with their far greater resources, soon outstripped them. In 1645, embittered by the endless delays and difficulties that always attended trading with the Persians, they massed their ships in the Persian Gulf and so won further concessions from the Shah (Abbas II). When, five years later, the Portuguese were driven from Muscat and their power in the Gulf finally broken, the rivalry between the English and the Dutch came to a head in Persia as well as in Europe. This time it was to be a new common enemy, France, who forced them to compose their differences.

The English factory in Isfahan was a palace, just to the west of the Qaisariyeh bazaar, which had been confiscated by Abbas from his chief town crier—an important official who had fallen from favour. Chardin, who was often a guest there, describes it in some detail. It consisted of three separate buildings set in a fine garden with large pools, but by his day (c. 1670) the place was rapidly falling into ruins. Trade was at this time bad, and the palace served principally as a kind of

49. Khwaju Bridge, built in the mid-seventeenth century, which serves both as a bridge and a dam.

summer station for the refreshment of the parboiled factors at Gombroon—a place of which Fryer wrote that only an inch-board of deal separated it from hell. Chardin says that it was the greatest pity that the buildings had been allowed to decay, because the painted and gilded ceilings were very fine indeed.

The site of the factory has been identified by Dr Lockhart with local help. It is now a caravanserai known as the Timcheh-yi-Firangi-ha or 'Little Caravanserai of the Franks', and stands at the end of an alley that runs westwards from the main part of the Qaisariyeh bazaar about 300 yards from the Maidan entrance.

The life of the factors must have been far more agreeable in Isfahan than in Gombroon, where the bad climate was responsible for much heavy drinking of punch, and a high mortality; there is, however, a pleasant description of a carouse in Isfahan, related by a man named Jefferis, at which one of the party drank until he was 'bereaved of footmanship' and had to be carried out.

The Dutch factory was a little to the north of its English counterpart, but the exact position is no longer known; de Bruyn gives two pictures of it and its pleasant and well-kept garden shaded by tall *chinars*. Its situation was, however, less favourable than that of the English factory, being further from the Bazaars and on the fringes of the brothel district. But it must be remembered that for the Dutch Isfahan was not their principal factory; unlike the English, they retained their headquarters at Gombroon.

A full account of the imports and exports of both factories can be found in Dr Lockhart's *The Fall of the Safavi Dynasty*.[62] The principal goods exported by the English from Persia were silk and, especially later, goats' wool; but the range was wide and included carpets and textiles, semi-precious stones, leather-work and Shiraz wine. From England in exchange came cloth, clocks, and household goods such as cups, saucers and plates; and from India, ebony, coconut-oil and sugar. Dutch trade was in general somewhat similar, but the Dutch at that time had what was virtually a monopoly in spices and perfumes—both commodities much in demand in Persia.

There was, of course, incessant rivalry between the Dutch and the English, with the former, thanks to their greater wealth, generally victorious. In 1699, however, the English scored a great triumph when they were able to entertain Shah Sultan Husain in their factory. It seems that the Shah, happening one day to pass by the English factory, was impressed by its appearance (dilapidated though the building had by this time become) and expressed his desire to visit it with his women.

With the help and advice of Persian officials, the principal room of the palace was appropriately prepared for the great occasion. A throne was erected, rich carpets spread everywhere in the house and along the garden paths, and fruit and wine made ready:

> The English then retired from the Factory, and left the charge of it to women, with instructions to receive, with all possible solemnity, the Monarch, the Ladies of his Harem, by whom he was attended, leaving only three petitions, one apologising for the inadequate pomp, with which they could receive the Monarch; another praying directions might be given to the eunuchs, to prevent persons attempting, by means of holes in the buildings, to look at the King and his attendants; and a third, that as, on so honourable an occasion, they could not disturb his Majesty with their requests, he would be pleased to order the Ettiman Doulut [Itimad al-Daula] to receive them.[63]

The Shah was so delighted with his reception that he announced his intention of repeating his visit. In fact he did not come again; and possibly the English factor was somewhat relieved that he did not, for the first reception had cost the Company no less than £1,200. The outlay proved, however, to have been fully justified, for the Shah behaved very generously, giving both money and handsome presents and expressing his confidence in the English Company while snubbing the Dutch by refusing their request for permission to build a fort at Gombroon.

Though the French, through their Capuchin Fathers and their merchants, had had considerable contact with Persia during the first half of the seventeenth century, their Compagnie des Indes Orientales was not founded until 1664. For various reasons it was unsuccessful in opening up trade on any scale in Persia: the English and Dutch Companies intrigued against it, and the Frenchmen squabbled among themselves. The Fabre-Michel mission to Persia resulted in the Franco-Persian Treaty of 1708,[64] and there was an even more improbable Persian embassy to France a few years later.[65] In each of these missions a woman played an important and a disastrous role, the French envoy being accompanied by his scheming mistress disguised as a *cavalier*, and the Persian returning from Paris with his—the young Marquise d'Epinay—concealed in a perforated crate purporting to contain his devotional books. Both Fabre and the Persian envoy came to untimely ends before they reached home, the former dying of fever and the latter committing suicide.

The gradual decline of trade relations between Persia and the European powers, which corresponded with the gradual decline of the Safavid dynasty, is another long and complicated story which may also be read in Dr Lockhart's admirable book.

Fig. 16. Detail of tilework in the Friday Mosque.

The minor arts

FOR THOSE WHO are unable to visit Iran, its architecture and its landscape must remain known to them only from the photograph or the written word. Most of the country's minor arts—its illuminated manuscripts, calligraphy and miniature painting; its ceramics, book-binding and metal-work; its carpets and its silk fabrics—can be studied in the great museums and private collections of Europe and America even better than in Iran itself. So prominent are these so-called 'minor' arts in Iran that the term is positively misleading. In all these manifestations of the artistic impulse Isfahan played its part; but by the end of the sixteenth century, when it first became the metropolitan city, the great Persian renaissance (like its counterpart in Italy) had passed its zenith. The late flowering of the arts in Isfahan, splendid and dramatic though it was, lacked the purity of its earlier manifestations.

LATER SAFAVID MINIATURE PAINTING

In later Safavid painting we think perhaps first of the murals which decorate the walls of the palaces of Isfahan. But the art of the miniature was by no means dead, though by now it had become largely dissociated from the book. The two most important names of the reign of Abbas the Great are those of Aqa Riza and Riza Abbasi.

There is still much confusion over the identity of these two men. It seems probable that Aqa Riza was brought up in Meshed, where his father held office at the court of the Governor. About 1590 Abbas was shown portraits that Aqa Riza had made, but the Shah was at that time busy fighting the Turks and the Özbegs and could not attend to the arts. Later, however, he summoned the painter to his new capital and put him to work for the court. It is said that towards 1608 Aqa Riza grew idle and frittered away his time watching wrestling; most of his best painting probably dates from the last decade of the sixteenth century.

If it is difficult to make certain identification of Aqa Riza's work, his idiom is at all events clear enough. Many of his paintings show single figures in mannered postures and languid attitudes. Often they sway a little forwards, with knees slightly bent, in rhythms that curiously recall the ivory carvings of medieval Europe. The shoulders slope, the contour of the cheek is full as an infant's, and the lips part in a wistful smile.

Riza Abbasi was a dazzling draughtsman whose fluid, mannered line, with its thickened accents and spluttered termination, has the calligraphic brilliance which we associate with the work of Far Eastern artists; and no doubt there is direct influence through the Chinese artisans whom Abbas had summoned to his capital. Riza Abbasi often worked in monochrome heightened with gold, and his *oeuvre* includes portraits of Europeans and also erotic subjects. His penmanship is seen at its best in the famous Sarre sketchbook in the Freer Gallery in Washington. According to his pupil, Mu'in, Riza Abbasi died in 1635.

50. Youth with a flask of wine. A miniature painted *c.* A.D. 1590. Treasury, Topkapi Palace Museum, Istanbul.

With the establishment of the Safavid dynasty in Iran at the beginning of the sixteenth century, the political and cultural focus of the country moved westwards, carrying with it the textile arts that had flourished in eastern Iran, Samarqand and Herat under the Timurids. The fact that cotton and woollen goods of fine quality were already being produced in Isfahan in the fifteenth century is testified by their being considered suitable to send as gifts to the Emperor of China. Soon the silk industry became important also, as it did in all those parts of Iran where the mulberry could be successfully grown.

Since the earliest days of her history, Iran had been famous for her rich fabrics. Clothes were sumptuous; garden pavilions were hung with gorgeous materials; horses were superbly caparisoned. There were magnificent banners for use in war and in tournaments, and wonderful curtains and cushions in private houses; and it is amusing to note that, at least as early as the fifteenth century, door-curtains were looped back with sashes, a style later to become the fashion in the West.

On state occasions the roads were covered, sometimes for miles at a stretch, with brocades, cloths of gold and embroideries. In the home, a valued manuscript would be kept in a brocade case, and an important letter or gift might be wrapped in a piece of silk; and it is recorded that the entire text of a book of verses was woven. In the weaving of carpets Iranian craftsmen have never been surpassed. Much of this traditional splendour is represented in the miniatures of the fifteenth, sixteenth and seventeenth centuries.

Among the few weaver-designers of the reign of Abbas the Great who are known to us by name is the Yazdi, Ghiyath. Rich, cultured, a maker of verses and a collector, a wit and a reformed rake, he became a privileged member of the Shah's court, where he seems to have been allowed the liberty of making jokes, even in the Shah's presence, at the expense of his fellow courtiers. Many of the fabrics designed by Isfahan artists were probably executed at Yazd, the most important centre of production in the seventeenth century, or at Kashan.

Shafi, son of Riza Abbasi and court painter to Abbas II, was famous for bird and flower drawings which often served for fabric designs. The output of fabrics such as brocades, compound twill with a metal thread ground, taffetas and velvets must have been enormous in Isfahan in the seventeenth century, and some idea of their incredible richness, delicacy and range can be gauged from the plates in the sixth volume of Professor Pope's great *Survey of Persian Art*.

CARPETS

Persian knotted carpets were among the first artistic exports from Iran to the West. Their beauty made an immediate impression upon diplomats and travellers, who found them at once the most desirable and the most portable products of the country. From the fifteenth century onwards there is record of Persian rugs in Europe; they are mentioned in the inventories of the possessions of Jean duc de Berry, Robert Earl of Leicester (1588), Cathérine de Medicis (1589) and other early collectors, and they figure in the paintings of Rubens and of many Italian and Dutch artists of the Renaissance. It was generally agreed that they were finer than those made in Cairo. Like the architects of the great Gothic cathedrals, the designers of these miraculous works of art were, more often than not, anonymous; and though a few carpets are signed, and some even dated, no carpet-designer is mentioned by name in the literature of the period.

51. Dome of the College of the Mother of the Shah (early eighteenth century).

52. Courtyard of the College of the Mother of the Shah.

Every Persian house, wrote Thomas Herbert, had its rugs; and often it was evident that they had been designed exactly to fit a given wall. Many were also made as royal gifts for an especially revered mosque or shrine; and really splendid examples were kept rolled up, like the *kakemonos* of the Far East, and only displayed on important occasions. But every devout Muslim had his own prayer-mat, marked with the niche that would be turned towards Mecca at the hours of prayer; and such rugs would be of the finest quality that their owners could afford.

Carpet-making was a tent-industry, a home-industry and a palace-industry. We learn, from Tavernier, that woven rugs (and doubtless knotted rugs also) were made on looms in Safavid times in Isfahan in the palace grounds behind the Ali Qapu. The water of Isfahan contained lime and it is therefore probable that most of the materials were dyed in more favoured localities and manufactured in Isfahan. That this was so is borne out by information given by Chardin, who speaks of large warehouses in Isfahan where wool and silks were stored.

One of the principal centres of carpet-making from the reign of Abbas the Great onwards was Joshaqan Qali ('Joshaqan the carpet-[town]'), about sixty-five miles to the north-west of Isfahan. The magnificent series of floral carpets designed for the tomb chamber of Abbas II at Qum were made here in 1661. Joshaqan was a popular summer resort of the courtiers in Safavid times, and traces of some of their palaces can still be seen. Many carpets were also made at Kashan.

As one would expect, the carpets made for Abbas the Great were large in scale and grandiose in design. The 'vase' carpets—also, and more reasonably, called 'Shah Abbas' carpets—contain great palmettes, huge leaves, flower-strewn meadows, and sometimes animals. The so-called 'Polonaise' carpets, most of which have found their way to Europe, were enriched with threads of silk, gold-covered silver, and silver. The colours are incredibly rich and infinitely varied. These carpets were used to cover floors and tables and to decorate walls; and Tavernier states that even the royal hunting cheetahs were allowed to lie upon them. So jealously was the secret of this particular kind of silk and silver thread embellishment preserved, that it was lost, so Krusinski tells us, at the time of the Afghan invasion when so many thousands of Isfahanis perished.

In the Victoria and Albert Museum, London, is a remarkable chasuble made of silk carpet with, in the centre, a representation of the Crucifixion. This was no doubt executed at Abbas the Great's command for the Armenians of Julfa, with whom he was often on the friendliest terms.

CERAMICS

Few would attempt to claim that Safavid pottery could stand comparison with the splendid wares produced several hundred years earlier in Ray, Sultanabad and elsewhere in Iran; yet under the Safavids there was a notable renaissance in the potter's art, which reached its culmination in the reign of Abbas the Great.

Abbas is said to have summoned to his capital 300 Chinese potters, and the most characteristic wares of his reign show the strong influence, and often the direct imitation, of Far Eastern ceramics. Probably Kerman was the centre for the manufacture of wares with a white siliceous body, in parts almost as translucent as porcelain. The colours are often delicate and subtle—pale slate, lavender, aubergine, rose, primrose and palest green. At other times we find intense blue, the bole-red that was so successfully used by the Iznik potters, and the celadon-greens of the Far East. One type of pottery carries figure-subjects closely related to the paintings of Aqa Riza and Riza Abbasi; and these same subjects are also to be found on tile-paintings, of which there are fine examples in the Chihil Sutun and the Victoria and Albert Museum, London. New forms were devised—large saucer-shaped rice dishes, little octagonal trays, long-necked perfume sprinklers, and so on. In short, the seventeenth century made a considerable contribution to the long history of the ceramic art in Iran.

GARDENS

One minor art remains to be mentioned, and one which only those who have visited Iran can appreciate: the art of the garden.

To those familiar with the great gardens of Europe, a Persian garden may at first seem disappointing. Tavernier wrote:

> You must not imagine that these are so curiously set out nor so well kept as ours in Europe. For they have no such lovely borders, nor such close walks of honeysuckles and jasmin as are to be seen in the gardens of Europe. They suffer the grass to grow in many places; contented only with a good many great fruit trees, tufted atop, and planted in a line, which is all the grace of the gardens of Persia.

The essential ingredients of a Persian garden are, of course, shade and water; today, there are usually few flowers other than roses and a handful of the more commonplace annuals.[66] But after the heat and the dust and the glare of the mid-summer streets, a cool and shady retreat is more than enough. Herbert, who must have been familiar with some of the great gardens of England and France, found those in Isfahan rewarding by any standards:

' Gardens here for grandeur and fragour are such as no city in Asia outvies ', he wrote, ' which at a little distance from the city you would judge a forest, it is so large; but withal so sweet and verdant that you may call it another paradise '. The finest of these was the Hazarjarib, which was situated beside the Chahar Bagh in its continuation on the southern bank of the Zayandeh-rud. Herbert considered the Hazarjarib ' deservedly famous ', but an orchard rather than a garden. He describes it as being about three miles in circumference, and approached by three wide and well-built gateways. A long avenue, which reminded him of Fontainebleau, revealed the full extent of the grounds. There was a large twelve-sided pool with an elaborate fountain in the centre of it, and a six-roomed pleasure pavilion, also furnished with a pool, which was decorated in the same manner as the Ali Qapu. The water was brought from a considerable distance by means of pipes.

Some Georgians invited Herbert to a party in this pavilion and, to his disgust, got very drunk; but there was consolation in the fact that Georgians never became quarrelsome in their cups. What he most enjoyed was the pastoral beauty of the place and the splendid view that the pavilion commanded of all Isfahan spread at their feet.

The later Safavids

' WHEN SHAH ABBAS THE GREAT ceased to breathe, Persia ceased to prosper '.

So wrote Chardin. But the impetus that Abbas had given to the dynasty was so great, that another century passed before it finally came to a close. Four more Safavid Shahs, all but one of whom were men of straw, ruled between the death of Abbas and the invasion of the Afghans in 1722: Shah Safi (1629-42), Shah Abbas II (1642-66), Shah Sulaiman (1666-94) and Shah Sultan Husain (1694-1722, d. 1726). Two puppet Safavid Shahs, Tahmasp II (1729-32) and Shah Abbas III (1732-6), ruled in little more than name.

SHAH SAFI (1629-42)

Abbas the Great, for all his many fine qualities, was responsible for the initiation— or perhaps the revival—of an evil practice which contributed very largely to the decline and fall of the Safavid dynasty: for fear lest his sons might conspire against him and attempt to usurp the throne, he kept them immured in the *anderun* (harem). Then, fearful that a measure of risk still remained, he put his eldest son to death and later blinded his two remaining sons, one of whom subsequently committed suicide. Thus the reins of government passed, and were to continue to pass, almost invariably into the hopeless hands of a callow boy or youth with no experience of the world. Abbas's three immediate successors—his grandson Safi, Abbas II, and Sulaiman—were respectively aged eighteen, nine, and eighteen when they ascended the throne.

Sir John Malcolm has neatly summarized the dangers attendant upon such a practice:

> A monarch, who was never permitted to leave this prison [i. e. the harem] till he ascended the throne, was likely to be effeminate and inefficient. It was hardly possible that he could resist the intoxication of absolute power. The unlimited indulgence of his passions seemed almost the certain consequence of his former privations, and his entire want of experience.[67]

Safi,[68] chosen by Abbas as his successor, was crowned in Isfahan on 5 February 1629. Father Dimas, then Vicar Provincial of the Carmelites, wrote to Rome later in the year to describe the various ceremonies that took place:

> During many days the king mounted a platform [plinth] at the gate of the palace, and the most distinguished persons went to kiss his feet. When one of them knelt down, the person concerned was held by Khusru Mirza and by-Baig, a leading personage and esteemed by the late Shah, after this fashion: the one took hold of the individual by the arm, the other by the other arm, and he was not released until he had withdrawn some little way. I omit much of the festivities they made of it in the Maidan, especially a *Chiraghani*—an illumination by candles, which lasted for three nights and which, they say, cost 3000 tomans and was paid for by the Banians [Hindu money-lenders and merchants] and other traders of the city.

Father Dimas also went in due course to pay his respects, offering the new Shah the quaintly assorted gifts of a letter from the Pope (which he had to take away again to make a translation), a copy of the Psalms in Arabic, and some water melons. He describes Safi as ' of fair height, and dignified presence; his face long, with large

53. Late sixteenth-century textile.
Victoria and Albert Museum, London.

eyes, and he is somewhat pitted with smallpox on the face which gives him a certain look. He is rather white in complexion, and shows many signs that he should succeed and rule with benignity and prudence ...' [69]

Strangely enough, Safi, though a drunkard, a drug addict and a brute, was consistently amiable to the Christians; for this reason, the anonymous author of *A Chronicle of the Carmelites in Persia* paints a more favourable picture of him than the facts appear to warrant. Father Krusinski's [70] portrait may stand: ' He meddled very little with affairs of the Government, passing his whole life with his bottle, his wives, or in hunting, so that had it not been for his numerous cruelties, which stained his reign with blood, it would have been scarce perceivable that he was ever King.' [71]

One of Safi's most reckless and cruel murders was that of Imam Quli Khan, the fine old Governor-General of Fars and conqueror of Hormuz, who was summoned to Isfahan and there slaughtered together with his three sons. Though warned that the Shah was angry with him, he counted upon his long years of faithful service to the throne and obeyed the order to present himself at court. Safi also ordered the killing of various princes and princesses of the blood royal, and all of his grandfather's most trusted ministers and generals. Thus the army command fell, and with disastrous results, into the hands of men almost as inexperienced as himself. In 1637 Kandahar was taken by the Mughal Emperor Shah Jahan, and the following year Baghdad was recaptured by the Turks, with whom Safi was forced to make a humiliating, but what proved however to be a durable, peace.

SHAH ABBAS II (1642-66)

In 1642, Safi set out to recover Kandahar from the Mughals. But he got no further than Qazvin where, according to the records of the East India Company's factory at Gombroon, he died of drink and debauchery. It is not impossible that he was poisoned.

His successor, Abbas II, being a mere child at the time of his father's death, escaped at an early age from the seclusion of the harem—which may well be the reason why he developed more favorably than any other of the later Safavids. A precocious boy, he showed, before he was fourteen, his virility by becoming a father and his good sense by poisoning his very meddlesome grandmother. Two years later, at the head of his armies, he recaptured Kandahar.

A certain austerity prevailed at court during the years of his minority, but in due course it became evident that though he possessed some at any rate of the good qualities of his great-grandfather and namesake, he had also inherited the Safavids' taste for alcohol and women. Malcolm wrote of him:

> The love of wine, in which this prince often indulged to excess, was the cause of all the evils of his reign. It was in his moments of intoxication alone that he was capricious, cruel, and unjust: but the danger from these excesses was in a great degree limited to the circle of his court; the country at large only knew this prince as one of the most generous and just rulers that ever reigned in Persia. To the public officers of government he was severe, but to the poor mild and lenient; and the lives and property of his subjects were efficiently protected. He was as tolerant to all religions as his great ancestor, whose name he had taken. To Christians, indeed, he always showed the most marked favour.[72]

SHAH SULAIMAN (1666-94)

Abbas II died in 1666 at the early age of thirty-three. An attempt on the part of his ministers to elect the Shah's younger son, still a mere child and therefore easy to handle, was frustrated by the loyalty of a eunuch. Abbas's elder son, the eighteen-year-old Safi, ascended the throne as ' Shah Safi '; but in 1669, because of certain

54. Polychrome tile mosaic.

sinister portents, he was recrowned as Shah Sulaiman. The circumstances which occasioned this second coronation were as follows:

Shortly after his accession the Shah had fallen ill. As a cure, his doctors recommended that a large sum of money should be collected from the inhabitants of Isfahan; this was then to be placed in a barrel and passed, every night for a whole week over the Shah's head. When this treatment had been tried, and tried again, without effect, the doctors changed their diagnosis and attributed his illness to the miscasting of his horoscope at the time of his accession. Therefore on a day proclaimed by the royal astrologers as unlucky, a mock coronation of a Zoroastrian was performed. Then, the following day (a lucky one), an effigy of the Zoroastrian was decapitated, and Shah Safi reassumed his throne as Shah Sulaiman.

Père Sanson described Sulaiman as tall and handsome, with large blue eyes, a Roman nose and a good complexion. In spite of a beard (which he dyed black) and a manly voice, there was something effeminate about him, and Sanson thought it a pity for a king not to have a more ' warlike air '. He was dignified yet affable, and there was ' a great deal of sweetness in his manner of speaking ... He is so very engaging, that when you bow to him he seems in some measure to return it, by a courteous inclination of his head, and which he always does smiling '.[74]

Sulaiman's harem upbringing had left him under the thumb of the Palace eunuchs. A wholesale slaughter of the nobility, court officials and military leaders, no doubt carried out at the instigation of the eunuchs, left the control of the state in the hands of these eunuchs and the men of their choice. Like all the Safavid Shahs, Sulaiman turned to women and wine, and Chardin reported that he could drink any Swiss or German under the table. He enjoyed making his ministers drunk because, *in vino veritas*, he was thus able to pick up information that they might have withheld from him when sober. His greatest pleasure was to see his guests carried out unconscious. Orders that he himself gave when in a drunken stupor were instantly carried out, however rash or brutal.

That Sulaiman's reign was for the most part peaceful was due to no merit of his, but to the fortunate fact that the Turks were occupied fighting in Europe. When ambassadors from European powers urged him to seize the opportunity to recover Baghdad, he replied that he intended to honour his treaty with the Turks. In view of the decadent state of his armies at this time, his decision was sound; but it was sloth and apathy, rather than common sense, which made him act as he did. When urged at least to build up his military strength so as to be ready to repel the Turks when they had made peace in Europe, he replied that they could do what they liked so long as they left him Isfahan.

SHAH SULTAN HUSAIN (1694-1722, d. 1726)

Shah Sulaiman had seven sons, most of whom appear to have been still living at the time of his death. Of these, Sultan Husain was the eldest and Abbas the second —young men of twenty-six and twenty-three years of age respectively, both brought up in the harem, both ignorant of the world, but in all other respects wholly different in character. The choice of a successor—for the Safavid Shahs felt themselves to be under no obligation to select the eldest—seemed to lie between them. On his deathbed, in 1694, Sulaiman summoned his ministers to the Palace and invited them to make the decision: ' If you want a warrior king ', he said, ' choose Abbas. If you want peace and ease, then choose Sultan Husain '.

It was Sulaiman's formidable aunt, Maryam, the sister of Abbas II, who received the first news of the Shah's death. Summoning the court eunuchs, she urged that Sultan Husain, who was her favourite great-nephew, should be chosen to succeed to the throne; and since a weak ruler also suited their books, they readily fell in with her wishes. In due course Sultan Husain was crowned in the Ayineh-khaneh Palace. A Franch missionary, Père Martin Gandereau,[75] has described the festivities held to celebrate the coronation—the illumination of the Maidan and the bazaars, and the parade, to the accompaniment of drums and trumpets, of the lions, leopards, elephants and other animals from the royal zoo. He continued: ' To judge from this display, it seems that they expect much of [Sultan Husain] '. If they did, they were soon to be sadly disillusioned.

From the waist upwards, Sultan Husain was a fine figure of a man: his face was attractive, his body well-formed. But the overall effect was marred by bow legs and splay feet. Hopelessly unathletic, he could not, at the time of his accession to the throne, even sit a horse. In character he was pious, humane, feeble; he has been called the Edward the Confessor of Persia. His piety earned him the nickname of ' Mulla Husain '; and another nickname, ' Yashki dir ', (' It is good '), was derived from his invariable reply of assent to every proposal made by the *mullas*. His good qualities were, in their effect, as disastrous as his weaknesses: his piety led him to place *mullas* in position of responsibility; his humanity made him abolish the death sentence, with the result that crime increased. His feebleness accelerated the decline of his country.

It was the fanatical and puritanical Shaikh Muhammad Baqir al-Majlisi, the dominant influence over the young Shah, who persuaded him, immediately after the coronation, to issue edicts forbidding wine-drinking, faction-fighting, and the apparently harmless sport of pigeon-flying, and to expel the Sufis [76] from the city. Six thousand bottles of wine were brought up from the royal cellars and poured out for all to see. The prohibition order caused consternation throughout the city, and most especially in court circles. Maryam was fond of the bottle, and the eunuchs had planned to make a drunkard of Sultan Husain in order to guarantee that he would not interfere in the government of the country. They hatched a plot: Maryam was to feign illness, and the royal physicians were ordered to declare that only wine could save her life. Wine was procured (from the Polish envoy), but Maryam refused to touch it unless her nephew drank first from the cup. Sultan Husain did —and found it delicious: so delicious, indeed, that he ordered a couple more bottles for himself, and was soon drunk. Maryam recovered, prohibition was abolished, Sultan Husain became a dipsomaniac, and the decline of the country gained momentum.

A horror of shedding blood is a quality so rare among oriental monarchs of all ages, as to set Sultan Husain apart from the rest of his race. Krusinski, who says that the Shah never passed a single death sentence in all his reign, relates that on one occasion Sultan Husain, when firing a pistol over the heads of a number of duck swimming on a pond in the Palace gardens, in order to make them take off but not to hurt them, was unlucky enough to wound several of them. He was as terrified as if he had committed murder, calling out, ' I am polluted with blood! ' and immediately gave 200 *tomans* to the poor in atonement for his sin.

Alexander Hamilton, a merchant who spent thirty-five years in various parts of the Middle East, relates a story which shows how hopelessly unfit was the Shah to rule, even in times of peace. News was brought to the Palace of a serious attack by the Özbegs on the north-east frontiers of his kingdom. The Vizier demanded an immediate audience with his master. But Sultan Husain happened at that moment to be playing with a young kitten, making it chase a feather tied to a piece of string; he sent word that he would see the minister later. ' But ', wrote Hamilton, ' he never thought more of it '.[77]

Sultan Husain was reckless with money. The cost of upkeep of the royal harem in his reign was treble the amount it had been under his predecessor, and the year

1700, when an organized search was instituted to gather in every pretty girl in his kingdom, was long remembered in Persia as ' *Kizlarun Ili* '—' the Year of the Girls '. Each girl had her personal eunuch and maid, and was given a handsome dowry when the time came for her to be married off.

Costly too were the great banquets held in the Chihil Sutun, during one of which, in January 1706, the hall suddenly caught fire and the building was badly damaged. It is said that Sultan Husain, considering the conflagration to be an ' act of God ', refused to allow any attempt to extinguish the flames. Father Peter Martyr, a Dominican, mentions the curious fact that among the pictures burnt were some representing ' Christ our Lord and the Blessed Virgin ', and that after the rebuilding of the Chihil Sutun Husain commandeered for its decoration an ' Assumption of the Virgin ' and a ' St Dominic ' which had been brought from Europe for the Dominican church.

Sultan Husain's piety involved him in even greater expense than his lechery. A pilgrimage to Meshed, accompanied by his entire harem and a train of 60,000 men, not only completely drained his exchequer, but also ruined all the provinces through which he passed.[78]

There was also his building—' his chiefest delight '. We are told that Sultan Husain demolished a fine palace in the Royal Gardens and erected a new one regardless of cost. But his vastest project in Isfahan—or rather, on its outskirts—was the Palace of Farahabad (' Abode of Joy '), near Julfa. Of this enormous building nothing now remains beyond broken walls, which confirm that its size was not exaggerated by historians. Dubeux, writing about 1840, saw a ruined pavilion which contained monochrome murals, painted in blue, showing several processions of all the animals known in Persia, from the lion to the rat, marching two by two as though into the Ark. Each procession terminated in two hooded Capuchins with hands crossed on their breasts. There is evidence that the Palace itself had little to commend it beyond its size; the great attraction of the Abode of Joy was its position at the foot of the Kuh-i-Suffa, and its splendid terraces, lakes and gardens.[79]

55. Mirror mosaic in the entrance to the Chihil Sutun.

55

Building and feasting under
the later Safavids

AFTER THE DEATH of Abbas the Great, his successors continued to embellish Isfahan. Though the quantity of buildings erected decreased, their quality showed little if any decline; indeed, many people consider the Khwaju Bridge, dating from the middle of the seventeenth century, and the College of the Mother of the Shah, completed only a few years before the Afghan invasion brought the great Safavid dynasty to its inglorious close, to be among the most attractive buildings that survive from that splendid era.

It has often been stated that the Safavid Shahs had 300 palaces in Isfahan alone. Chardin gives us the explanation: the Shah, he wrote, possessed 300 *houses* in Isfahan; when ambassadors or other distinguished visitors arrived in the capital, one or more of these houses would be put at their disposal. The remainder, almost always empty, gradually fell into disrepair. There were, however, a large number of Safavid palaces, both in Isfahan itself and elsewhere in Iran; but only a handful of these has survived. In Isfahan are the Ali Qapu, the Talar Ashraf, the Hasht Bihisht, and—finest of all—the Chihil Sutun. The charming Ayineh-Khaneh (Hall of Mirrors) has vanished without trace (but for a few stone bases of columns scattered about the gardens of the Chihil Sutun). It was destroyed towards the end of the last century by the Zil es-Sultan, the Qajar Governor of Isfahan who had conceived a hatred for the Safavids; on the site there is now a textile factory. Vanished too are the Imarat Bihisht, so enthusiastically described by Chardin and others, and the Haft Dast ('Seven Perfections' built by Tahmasp II in a garden on the outskirts of the city; very probably the Zil was once again responsible.[80]

THE CHIHIL SUTUN

The Chihil Sutun is situated in the Royal Park, behind the Ali Qapu; it was a ceremonial palace designed for state occasions and particularly for the reception of foreign embassies. The building was long believed to date from the time of Abbas the Great, but in the course of restoration carried out in 1948 an inscription was found recording its completion in 1647 under Abbas II; probably, however, the core of the palace dates from the beginning of the century.

Though Chihil Sutun means 'Forty Columns', the *talar* of the palace has no more than twenty, two of these being in the recess which constitutes the Throne Room. Alternative explanations are offered for this anomaly: that the reflections of the columns in the large rectangular pool in front of the Palace brings the number up to forty; or that 'chihil' is a common term in Persian to indicate a large but imprecise number. An earlier building in Samarqand had been named Chihil Sutun; the Chihil Dukhtaran ('forty daughters') minaret in Isfahan has already been mentioned; and there was of course Ali Baba and his forty thieves. It can hardly be doubted that the 'reflection' theory, though picturesque enough to be oriental, is in fact no more than an ingenious occidental invention.

By western standards the Chihil Sutun is a small building, yet the height (forty-eight feet) and elegance of the slender columns of the *talar* give it grandeur. The

56. The Hasht Bihisht, a small pleasure pavilion in the grounds of the Royal Palace (seventeenth century).

Fig. 17. The Chihil Sutun (from *La Perse*, by Mme Dieulafoy, 1887).

ceiling of the *talar* is magnificent, and the casualness and informality of the construction—nothing is quite horizontal or quite vertical—add greatly to the charm
of the ensemble. The columns, stripped now of their original looking-glass veneer,
are painted red; four of them rest upon stone bases carved in the form of lions,
the remainder upon undecorated bases. Originally there were curtains which could
be lowered to within eight feet of the ground to provide shade and coolness in the
summer months.

Until relatively recently the whole of the façade of the Chihil Sutun, under the
talar, was covered with mirror-mosaic; it now survives only in the recess. This
conceit, which was to become very popular under the Qajars, was originally devised
(or so it is alleged) as a cunning device for making use of the fragments of the many
mirrors which were broken during the long journey from Europe; it was developed
by the Persians into a brilliant feature of architectural decoration. These Persian
mirror rooms find their nearest European equivalent in the glittering *Spiegelsäle* of
Bavarian rococo palaces or of Ludwig II's fabulous *Schloss* at Linderhof. The Persians employed mirror-mosaic both in religious and in secular buildings, the Shrine
of the Imam Reza at Meshed, the Mosque at Qum and the Gulistan Palace in Tehran
being among the most impressive examples in Iran. The exact date of the first room
to be decorated in this way is uncertain. The use of mirrors on the columns of
the *talar* of the Chihil Sutun certainly dates from the seventeenth century, and Chardin refers to ' *chassis de cristal, de toutes couleurs* ' in the audience hall; but it is possible that the mirror-mosaics of the throne recess were added during the rebuilding
after the great fire in 1706 when part of the palace was destroyed (*see* p. 130).

134

A number of little rooms, delightfully decorated with Safavid figure-paintings in varying state of disrepair and renovation, and designed for the use of the Shah and his ministers, open out of the *talar*.   On each side of the mirrored recess small, shabby doors lead to the main audience hall, now used as a museum.

The ceiling of this great room is probably the finest surviving example of its kind in Iran.   Plaster-work in low relief is sumptuously decorated in ultramarine and cobalt blue, vivid scarlet, pale emerald, and solid gold—the whole woven into intricate and exquisite patterns of great richness.   It is in a good state of preservation, and restoration, where necessary, has been most judiciously carried out.

The same cannot, alas, be said of the series of large and interesting decorative seventeenth- and eighteenth-century oil paintings which cover the main walls of the hall.   But, heavy and graceless and mutilated though they are, enough remains for their subject-matter to be clearly intelligible.   Shah Tahmasp is shown receiving an ambassador from the Great Moghul, Abbas the Great defeats the Özbegs, Nadir Shah captures Delhi, and so on.   The treatment is more Westernized than in miniature paintings of similar themes;   indeed Western artists may have had a part in them.   The pictures also provide valuable information on matters of detail, such as the instruments played by the musicians, the dresses worn, the food served at banquets, and so on.

In display-cases round the hall are manuscripts, costumes, tiles, metal vessels, and

Fig. 18.   The Palace of Mirrors (from *La Perse*, by Mme Dieulafoy, 1887).

the like. These cases, ugly in themselves, and the whitewash that surrounds them, distract the eye and disturb the homogeneity of the wall surfaces; one turns again and again to the beauty of the ceiling, leaving the imagination to reclothe the walls and floor with the Safavid arabesques and fine carpets which they once wore. Fortunately, small portions of these arabesques, very similar in character to those in the Ali Qapu, survive on the end walls of the hall and provide a clue to the original decoration.

The gardens of the Chihil Sutun—almost all that now remains of the vast park in which the royal palaces were situated—are delightful. They too are in the process of becoming a museum, for against the northern boundary wall the handsome but much restored portal of the Qotbiyeh Mosque (1543) has been re-erected, and elsewhere are further examples of tile-work from other mosques in and around Isfahan.

On the external side-walls of the Chihil Sutun are other Safavid wall-paintings. One of these shows what may possibly be King Charles I of England and his Queen, Henrietta Maria, and was no doubt carried out by a Persian artist using a European painting or engraving. Another is a portrait of a European envoy, probably also an Englishman, holding in his hand a vegetable which perhaps is a turnip; the Persians always welcomed the gift of unfamiliar plants.[81]

FEASTING IN THE CHIHIL SUTUN

Such are the dry bones of the Chihil Sutun; let us break away for a moment from architecture and try to bring them to life by describing three of the innumerable feasts which were held there under the last monarchs of the Safavid dynasty. On each of these occasions some of the Franks were present.

Abbas II liked the Franks: they amused him; they were excellent boon-companions. Early in the year 1665 he had made an important and profitable deal with Tavernier, from whom he had purchased 60,000 crowns' worth of jewels. He felt in the mood for carousing. So he held two feasts, at both of which Tavernier, and a protégé of his who had accompanied him to Persia, a man named André Daulier-Déslandes, were present. Both these men described what passed;[82] their accounts differ in detail, each author alleging that it was *he* who was the life and soul of the party, but they agree in substance.

Daulier-Déslandes was not invited to the first feast, but was sent for during the course of it. Before eight o'clock in the morning Tavernier was summoned to the Palace, where he found Father Gabriel, two Dutchmen and one or two other Frenchmen already waiting in the ante-room. After the usual delays they were conducted into the presence of the Shah, who was seated upon a rich carpet on a low dais, and leaning against a cushion four feet in length. In front of him stood dishes of fruit and sweetmeats; and there were also two tall Venetian glass bottles, filled with Shiraz wine and stoppered with pitch, for his private use. For his guests there was a large bowl of the same wine, which was doled out with a golden ladle into golden cups.

'Are you going to drink, or aren't you?' the Shah asked Father Gabriel. 'For if not, then you can go.' The poor Father, who was a teetotaller, reluctantly agreed to drink 'in moderation'. One of the Dutchmen was ordered to pour out the wine: it was his first experience of a feast of this kind; he had already earned a sharp rebuke for taking off his hat (a social solecism), and his hand trembled. 'The great ladle went about very smartly, considering it was but early in the forenoon', wrote Tavernier. Then the Shah recollected that the Franks were not used to drinking on an empty stomach, and ordered food to be brought in.

57. Minaret and dome
of the College of the Mother
of the Shah
(early eighteenth century).

First a *sofreh* (table-cloth) was spread out and covered with a length of leather, upon which was laid an enormous piece of bread, paper-thin and the same size as the *sofreh*, to serve as a top table-cloth.   For food there were pilaus of chicken and meat (grilled rather than roasted), two-foot loaves of delicious bread, lemons from Mazandaran and pomegranates from Shiraz.   Everyone made a hearty breakfast.

Then the Shah cross-examined Tavernier about his various travels and asked him how many princes he knew by sight.   A satchel containing miniature paintings was brought in, and the Frenchman had no difficulty in recognizing Shah Jahan, Aurang-

Fig. 19.   Throne Room in the Chihil Sutun (from *La Perse*, by Mme Dieulafoy, 1887).

58. Silver door, College of the Mother of the Shah (early eighteenth century).

zeb, and other Indian emperors. 'Take this one and keep it,' said Abbas, handing him the picture of a Persian woman; 'then your French women will be able to see how our women dress.' Two oil paintings of Venetian courtesans were next produced, and Tavernier invited to make his choice between them. 'Do you prefer blondes or brunettes?' asked Abbas. 'Sire,' replied Tavernier; 'were I to buy women as I purchase diamonds, pearls and bread, I would always choose the whitest.' The Shah was delighted and—a great honour—offered him wine from his own cup.

The conversation then turned on more serious subjects—politics, the state of Europe, and so on. After a while a troupe of dancing girls, who had been feasting in an adjoining room, were ordered to perform. Tavernier, who had noticed how heavily they had been drinking, was astonished to discover that they appeared to be perfectly sober. A small orchestra accompanied the dancing, the rhythm being accentuated by an old woman who played upon 'a large unsightly tambourine... There was also a little Georgian boy who played quite nicely on the harp, and an Armenian who made a great din on an organ that had been presented to the Shah.' The dancers did not join hands, but swayed their arms and bodies, singing as they did so.

More playing, more dancing and more drinking induced 'a surprising degree of familiarity' between the Shah and his guests. 'Which of the girls do you think the prettiest?' asked the Shah. Tavernier rose, took a candle and closely inspected each in turn; then, discreetly, he picked out what appeared to be the oldest. Abbas was puzzled: 'Why not *that* one?' he asked, pointing to a very pretty young girl. 'Well, each of them shall kiss you, and you will notice the difference.' The experiment was performed; but Tavernier still stuck to his opinion, saying that prudence accompanied age. 'Then take her home with you,' said Abbas. Tavernier refused: 'I have a wife in France,' he said, 'and I've never been unfaithful to her yet.'

After they had 'thus drolled together' for fourteen hours, Abbas inquired whether there was anyone present who could play upon a Dutch spinet which had just been presented to him. Father Raphael mentioned Daulier-Déslandes's name, and a messenger was sent post-haste to fetch him.

Poor Daulier-Déslandes had been hunting all day; he was just about to snatch a mouthful of food and then go straight to bed, when the messenger arrived at the Augustinian Convent, where he was lodging, and bore him off at full speed on the crupper of his horse. 'He did not give me a moment to collect my wits,' he lamented.

At this point the accounts of Daulier-Déslandes and Tavernier differ. According to Daulier-Déslandes, he

> ... played, or rather 'banged,' some chords and, although the spinet was out of tune, and I played nothing worth hearing, I managed to please the Shah, who said it was good. But, as I knew differently, and could not hear myself for the noise, I suggested singing a drinking song. The Shah approved and, since I could think of nothing more suitable to Shrovetide, which it happened to be, and to the occasion, I sang the song which runs: 'Heigh for Shrove Tuesday! the feast for all jolly drunkards.'

The other Franks joined in the chorus 'in an absurd manner', one of them using his hat as a megaphone.

According to Tavernier, however, Daulier-Déslandes 'pretended to sing', and in a squeaky tenor which sounded ridiculous to the Persians who are mostly bass. So Tavernier, who was totally unmusical but whose voice was a deep bass, came to the rescue and scored a great success with an old French air about the relative merits of women and wine. The Shah cried out, 'The works of God! the works of God!'—the equivalent of 'Bravo!', and demanded an encore.

59. Youth with narcissus. A miniature of the seventeenth century Isfahan School, painted in the style of Aqa Riza. *Treasury, Topkapi Palace Museum, Istanbul.*

عجب نیست و تاب افتاده در لطف بمنجو زنجرش

مکر دوست قضا زیده در نگام تحریرش

The unfortunate Daulier-Déslandes had eaten nothing since noon; he had arrived at the Palace to find dinner cleared away and steady drinking compulsory. So he appealed to Tavernier, who succeeded in finding him an apple; and another Frenchman unearthed a slice of cake. These he gratefully ate, then drank cup for cup with the others; after all, he was still a great many cups behind.

Soon after midnight the major-domo, observing that the guests were nodding, pointed this out to the Shah, who dismissed them. Tavernier was thankful to make his escape; he had been there, sitting on his heels, for nearly seventeen hours.

The second party, held a few days later, followed much the same pattern as the first, but it got more out of hand and ended in tragedy. Quite early on, one of the Frenchmen, who was playing the fool while Daulier-Déslandes was playing the spinet, dropped a bottle of wine on the instrument and put it out of action. A very drunk Persian was present. When the Shah ordered him to drink more wine, he refused. He was then offered water in the hat of one of the Frenchmen; this too he refused, so his turban was removed and the water was poured over his head.

> Then—and I do not know what possessed him to do it—the Shah took the Persian by the leg and pulled him towards him so roughly that he cried aloud. The Shah untied his garter, pulled off his stocking and, taking hold of his foot, bit it so severely that the poor wretch shrieked. We were much at a loss to know the meaning of all this, but what followed showed us that it meant mischief to the man who, having added other extravagancies to his previous follies, was driven out by the Shah, who ordered his ears to be cut off. In fact, even worse happened, for we were told next day that he had been beaten to death.

By now the whole room was strewn with broken glass. This gave the Shah the idea of making the dancers dance barefoot; it amused him to see them cutting their feet. The Franks, who had had more than enough of this horseplay, were grateful when permission was given for them to withdraw and return to their lodgings.

Such were the orgies that took place in the Chihil Sutun under the seventeenth-century Safavid Shahs. The informality of these feasts is in strong and unexpected contrast with the ceremonial pomp of an entertainment given by Shah Sultan Husain—unexpected, because Sultan Husain was almost as heavy a drinker as his drunken father, Shah Sulaiman.

In the spring of the year 1721, Bishop Barnabas of Isfahan was summoned to the Chihil Sutun to present to Shah Sultan Husain certain letters which had arrived from Europe. After the documents had been handed over ' according to the ceremonial already explained on other occasions,' two stools ' in the European style '— a novelty at this time—were brought for the Bishop and his companion. The Bishop's was placed

> ... as it were opposite the King, but at a distance of twelve or fourteen paces, for between the Shah and myself there was a beautiful fountain. The stool for my companion was placed eight or ten paces behind mine, and at a different elevation from that where were all the principal fellow-guests, being three or four steps lower.

Bishop Barnabas describes the *talar*, which today remains structurally as it was then but for the stripping of much of its mirror-mosaic:

> The place where the King held his reception is not a room or covered hall, but a very large open porch, handsomer and more majestic than that of St. Peter's, though not so big. It is completely full of large and small mirrors, marvellously interlaced, and some pictures with fine frames. There are in it twenty-four [sic] columns, the shafts of which must be of wood, but externally are altogether covered with small pieces of looking-glass like the whole porch, which is full of very rich couches, some of them of gold. In the middle of the porch, inside, as it might be the great door of St. Peter's, there is a large niche where is the King, sitting on a big cushion of brocade with another behind his shoulders.

Then the feast was served, and with as much decorum as at a banquet today:

> When, therefore, we had sat down on our stools they brought me a great tray of comfits and other sweetmeats. A little later they brought water spiced with cinnamon and sugar to the Shah, who after drinking a small coffee-cup sent one to me. A quarter of an hour later they began to spread the cloths for the dinner, and one of brocade, as were the rest, was laid in front of me. They carried the foodstuffs first to the King: there were fifteen to twenty valets, each with a royal dish, some of the dishes being of gold, others of majolica from China or, as we should say, porcelain; but all the dish-covers were of gold. The first dish was so large that it might rather be termed a great pot of gold, very heavy with its companion lid, and was borne by two valets because one alone could not carry it.
>
> To each of the guests, as to myself, they brought seven royal dishes, four of gold and three of majolica, but all with a great golden lid and brim-full of many kinds of food. The King began to eat, and all the rest were eating, so I was obliged to do likewise. The meal lasted about half-an-hour, but was so well ordered, and with such ceremony and absence of noise, that it seemed like a refectory full of monks. When the meal was at an end, the cloths were taken away and they brought round gold and silver jugs and basins for us to wash our hands. Then all rose and each went his way, as also did I, having first bowed to the Shah.[83]

TALAR ASHRAF

In another part of what was once the Royal Gardens stands an unpretentious three-*ivan* pavilion—the Talar Ashraf. The simple exterior is in strong contrast to the richness of the decorations within; these, bold in design, curiously anticipate the wall-papers and printed fabrics of William Morris. There are also some fine ceilings. Russian troops were stationed in the Talar Ashraf during the First World War, but the decorations, covered at that time by coats of whitewash, suffered no damage and today are for the most part in a very good state of preservation.

THE HASHT BIHISHT

In the Chahar Bagh, almost opposite to the College of the Mother of the Shah, there stands an ornate blue gateway at present kept closed; this will soon give access to the former Bagh-i-Bulbul, or 'Garden of the Nightingale', in which stands the little Hasht Bihisht ('Eight Paradises') Palace.[84] This little pleasure pavilion has recently been acquired by the State, and after restoration will be thrown open to the public.

The Palace, erected by Shah Sulaiman about 1670, is a slightly octagonal building with deep *talars*, two of which lead into a central hall. Small rooms surround this on two levels. The whole building was so refashioned under Fath Ali Shah at the beginning of the last century that it is almost impossible to reconcile Dr Fryer's account of it, written in 1677, with its present appearance. Fryer states that it was entirely constructed of polished marble, the ceiling of the hall being of inlay work and solid gold and supported by columns covered with mirrors. On the wall were paintings of the great heroes of Persian history and legend, and under the ceiling was a pool made of silver. In the gardens were two canals on which miniature warships floated as if engaged in battle and where swans and pelicans disported themselsev.

Madame Dieulafoy, who saw the Hasht Bihisht in the 1880s, did not even realize that the building was Safavid, so completely had the Qajars altered it. It had already been stripped of its furnishings, but the wall decorations remained intact. These consisted principally of two large oil paintings: one of these showed Fath Ali Shah with some of his innumerable sons (he is said to have had 600); and the other represented the Shah transfixing a lion or a panther with his lance—' I can't say which,' wrote Mme Dieulafoy; ' the artist, very properly more concerned with the royal personage, neglected to draw the animal with precision ...'[85] Smaller

61. Tile mosaic on the base of the minaret of the Royal Mosque.

62. Detail of tile mosaic from the Lutfullah Mosque.

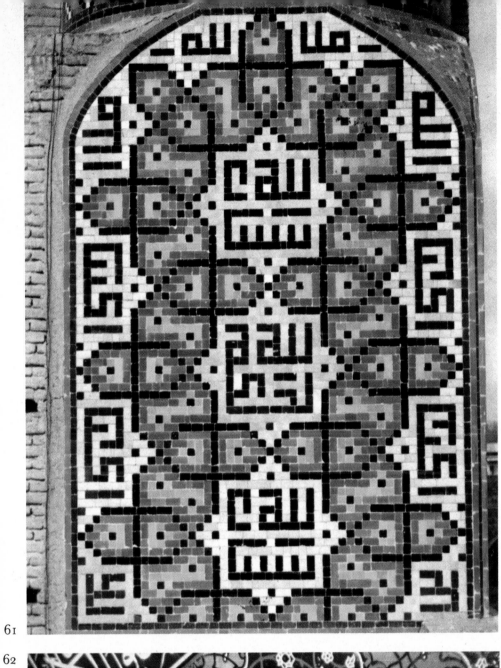

61

62

paintings included one of Strachey (' Istarji '), the English Adonis who accompanied Sir John Malcolm's Mission to Persia and whose wasp-waist made so deep an impression on Fath Ali Shah that he ordered his portrait to be painted for most of the royal palaces in Isfahan and Tehran.[86]

Mme Dieulafoy states that the pavilion earned its name from the eight little sets of apartments in which Fath Ali Shah, when in Isfahan, lodged his eight favourite mistresses of the moment; it may have served this purpose, but the name was already in use in the seventeenth century.

Today the building is crumbling and melancholy. The fittings have been looted, much of the decoration has perished or suffered defacement, hornets nest in the rafters. Only in one of the small upper rooms can one form any real impression of how very beautiful it all must once have been. Tile-work can be easily and invisibly repaired, but mural paintings present a much harder problem; the Department of Antiquities has an important, but a very difficult, task ahead.

THE IMARAT BIHISHT

Almost every later writer on Isfahan has assumed that this building, described in great detail by Chardin, is to be identified with the Hasht Bihisht. Undoubtedly it is of the same date; but Chardin was always precise with his measurements, and even a casual glance at his account makes it evident that the Imarat Bihisht (' Paradise Building ') was a *seven*-sided building, and very much larger; the shallow-domed ceiling of the central hall was 100 feet above the ground.

Chardin abandons his sober prose and becomes unaccustomedly lyrical in his description of the Imarat Bihisht:

> When one walks in this place expressly made for the delights of love, and when one passes through all these cabinets and niches, one's heart is melted to such an extend that, to speak candidly, one always leaves with a very ill grace. The climate without doubt contributes much towards exciting this amorous disposition; but assuredly these places, although in some respects little more than cardboard castles, are nevertheless more smiling and agreable than our most sumptuous palaces.[87]

Where was the Imarat Bihisht? Somewhere, no doubt, in the Royal gardens; but like several other such palaces known to us from the accounts of early travellers, it has vanished without trace.

THE KHWAJU BRIDGE

Though the Thirty-three-arch bridge is broader, and far longer, than the Khwaju, the latter is in the opinion of most people today the more attractive. Built by Abbas II in the middle years of the seventeenth century, probably to replace an earlier bridge that had become inadequate, the bridge linked the suburb of Guebristan directly with the town and so discouraged its Zoroastrian inhabitants from using the Thirty-three-arch bridge.

With its stone foundations and piers and its superstructure of brick, its open promenades and its pavilions, it follows the general pattern of its upstream rival. The Khwaju, however, is more than a bridge: it is also a dam, with great flights of stone steps pierced by narrow channels controlled by sluice-gates. Its peculiar charm depends upon the six semi-octagonal pavilions which, unlike those of the Thirty-three-arch bridge, are important enough to relieve the monotony of a long sequence of arches. Originally these pavilions were decorated and gilded and bore uplifting texts in prose and verse, one of which is cited by Chardin: ' The World

63. Detail of the tile-work from the College of the Mother of the Shah.

is truly a Bridge; pass over it. Weigh and measure all that you meet with on your passage. Everywhere Evil encompasses the Good and transcends it.' There were also erotic paintings which deeply shocked Sir William Ouseley when he saw them. These texts and decorations have long since disappeared, to be replaced by pretty but unimportant modern tile-work and painted arabesques.

Like the Chahar Bagh, the Khwaju bridge was once the evening resort of the citizens of Isfahan. 'In the evening,' wrote de Bruyn, 'you see an infinite number of persons of both sexes taking the air by the riverside, near the waterfall, and in the

Fig. 20. Lower Gallery of the Khwaju Bridge (from *La Perse*, by Mme Dieulafoy, 1887).

fine way that runs along the arches of the bridge, some on horseback, some on foot, smoking and drinking coffee, which they find ready prepared for them.'[88] Today, except when the melting of the mountain snows briefly transforms the innocent Zayandeh-rud into a spectacle, the place is frequented by few beyond a handful of washerwomen and idling children.

A SAFAVID PRIVATE HOUSE

A few private houses dating from Safavid times still remain in Isfahan; of these, that of the painter Hajji Musavvir al-Mulk is perhaps the most perfect example.

Round a little court, replete with its pool and pines and pomegranate tree, is a low building divided into tiny rooms decorated as exquisitely as those of the Ali Qapu and in a much better state of reapair. Every familiar feature of Persian rococo is there: the honeycombing, the floral arabesques, the glitter of gold, the mirror mosaics, the fretted niches—but all on what seems to be, after the palaces, a doll's-house scale. To see such a house inhabited is to be transplanted back to the days of Abbas II or Shah Sulaiman. Thus the courtiers of the Safavid Shahs must have lived—and one cannot but be envious of their gracious living.

Hidden in the labyrinth of the Bazaars and difficult to find is the Masjid-i-Hakim, or Doctor's Mosque, erected in 1654 at the expense of a certain Hakim Daoud. This man was royal physician to Shah Safi; but he fell foul of Safi's successor, Abbas II, and fled to India. There, at the court of Shah Jahan, he grew rich; and it was with the money which he sent back to his family in Isfahan that the mosque was built, to the glory of God and in Daoud's honour.

The mosque is entered through a pretty stalactite-roofed portal which leads to a very spacious and well-tended court showing many signs of restoration. There is a handsome pierced screen on the north-west side of the court.

In the Bazaars are also two Safavid *madrasehs*. That of Mulla Abdulla no longer serves as a school; but the Madraseh-yi-Sadr, with its most delightful pine-shaded garden, seems to be thriving, though it now contains little of architectural interest.

THE IMAMZADEH SHAH ZAID

There are also several other lesser mosques and *madrasehs* dating from the later part of the seventeenth century. But of these there is space to mention one only—the Imamzadeh Shah Zaid.

This small sanctuary, which is situated in a dusty suburb on the eastern fringes of the city, is one of the curiosities of Isfahan, for its wall are covered with figure paintings.[89] This is, of course, quite contrary to Muslim precepts; but there was always more freedom in those countries which belonged to the Shi'a sect of Islam.

The original building, and probably the fine buff dome patterned in turquoise and black, are early Safavid (c. 1585); but its unique interior was entirely remodelled, about 100 years later, under Shah Sulaiman. The paintings are crude but dramatic, and illustrate episodes in the life of Husain, the grandfather of Zaid. Warriors on horseback occupy the major part of the wall-space, but there is also much entertaining detail. There are veiled women, Franks, dead bodies; lions, gazelles and birds; tents and mosques; tulips and other flowers. The naive artist has filled every available square inch of space, and where there is insufficient room to introduce a major object he has slipped in an apple, a flagon or a cup. The prevailing colour is a rich chestnut brown.

The Imamzadeh is briefly mentioned by Chardin, who must have seen it shortly before its walls were painted.

THE THEOLOGICAL COLLEGE OF THE MOTHER OF THE SHAH
(MADRASEH-YI-MADAR-I-SHAH)

There are buildings which at first sight seem austere and forbidding, but whose formal beauty and fitness become apparent after careful study; and there are others which have a certain picturesqueness that sometimes proves to be beauty only skin deep. No one could enter the court of the College of the Mother of the Shah without immediately reacting to the overwhelming charm of the setting; yet familiarity with it does not breed contempt—rather an astonishment that anything so admirable in every way could have been produced at a moment when the Safavid dynasty was almost in its death throes. It has been described as the last construction that in any sense deserves the qualification of 'great' in Iran.

The Madraseh was built between the years 1706-14 at the expense of the mother of Shah Sultan Husain, as a training College for theological students. In Curzon's day it was still being used for its original purpose, though so large a part of the endowments had by then been embezzled by the government that only some 50 of the 160 chambers were occupied at that time. Today, though the place remains open for prayer, there are no students left. Curzon described it as one of the stateliest *ruins* that he saw in Persia; now brilliantly restored and a ruin no longer, it has become one of the most handsome, and possibly the most charming, of all the public monuments of Isfahan.

The Madraseh is entered from the Chahar Bagh through a stalactite-vaulted *ivan* in the centre of a long façade with blind arcading. The *ivan* is pleasant enough but in no way remarkable; the gates however, are made of wood covered with silver plates in part gilded and are unusually magnificent. The visitor passes first into a vaulted octagonal vestibule in which stands a huge stone basin for ritual ablutions, and thence into the main court. Here he is confronted, not with the customary large bleak acreage of paving-stones, but with a delightful garden shaded by tall, white-stemmed *chinars* and set about with pools and a long marble-edged tank. Only in the Shrine at Mahan, near Kerman, is anything comparable to be found in Iran; but in the Madraseh the charm is enhanced by the contrast between the noisy thoroughfare just left behind, and the exquisite peace and silence of the court. To a horticulturist the garden is nothing: mere ' bedding-out '; but anyone who has travelled in hot, noisy, arid, dusty countries can understand the solace afforded in Iran by the combination of such simple ingredients as shade, water, coolness, silence, and a handful of commonplace flowers.

The ensemble is immensely photogenic, and the click of the camera often breaks the silence; indeed, no less than five recently published books on Iran have a photograph of the Madraseh on their dust-jackets. The authorities allow visitors to climb up on to the roof, where they can obtain an endless variety of picturesque views of glittering tile-work seen through a silver filigree of *chinar* and mirrored in unruffled pools.

The main court of the Madraseh is rectangular, but cut across at each corner to give access to smaller courts where the officers of the College once lived. On the north side of the court is the domed Sanctuary, approached by a tall *ivan* topped by two minarets. All these follow the pattern of their counterparts in the Royal Mosque, but the scale is somewhat smaller and the proportions more elegant. The dome, with its huge and twining arabesques of black, yellow and white on a turquoise ground, and the drum with its contrasting band of lapis lazuli blue and its splendid calligraphic inscriptions, show no trace of decadence in design or execution; indeed, the ensemble of *ivan*, dome and minarets is as noble as any to be found in Iran.

Of the remaining *ivans*, one of course serves as entrance to the court; the other two were used as lecture halls for instruction in theology, Arabic grammar and literature, and elementary science. The remaining surface of the façades is broken by a succession of vaulted niches which lead into inner rooms where the students were lodged; it was in one of these rooms that Shah Sultan Husain spent the last night of his life before he was decapitated—probably in the College itself—by the Afghans. Everywhere the tile-work is gay and light-hearted, yet it is never vulgar; there is some enchantingly delicate tracery in the arcades.

Adjoining the Madraseh the Shah's mother also built a *khan*, or caravanserai, to provide revenue for its upkeep. Until recently this was occupied by the army; but it has now been transformed into a luxury garden for the new Shah Abbas hotel.

Only six years after the completion of the Madraseh and caravanserai, Isfahan was besieged and captured by the Afghans. How fortunate a fate that these last noble buildings were finished before this great calamity, and that they came through the holocaust without suffering irreparable damage!

64. Hunting carpet, seventeenth-century Isfahan workmanship. *Victoria and Albert Museum, London.*

The Afghans and Nadir Shah   Part 3

FOR MORE THAN twenty years, under the feeble rule of Sultan Husain, the country ran steadily yet peacefully into decline; then, suddenly, there was trouble on every hand. The Kurds revolted; the Özbegs revolted; the Arabs of Muscat seized the island of Bahrein and threatened the mainland, and the wild Afghans grew bold and insolent on the eastern frontiers. It was, as it happened, the Afghans [90] who were to bring about the downfall of the enfeebled Safavid dynasty, and a certain Mahmud was to be the instrument of its destruction.

The horror of the awful years that followed are passed over so lightly in most of those books which are offered to the tourist, that many leave the city unaware of the great calamity that overwhelmed it in 1722. But to write of Isfahan as if it were merely the prosperous capital of Shah Abbas, is as misleading as it would be to write of the splendours of Paris under Louis XIV with no more than a hint of the Revolution that was soon to follow. There are, indeed, not a few parallels between Versailles and Isfahan.

MAHMUD

Mahmud was a young man of nineteen when, in 1717, he murdered his uncle and seized power in Afghanistan. The Jesuit Father Krusinski, who five years later was to witness the Afghan's triumphant entry into Isfahan, has described his appearance. Mahmud was of medium height and stockily built, with a broad face, flat nose, blue eyes with a slight squint, and a scrap of carroty beard. His neck was so short that his head seemed to be set directly upon his shoulders. He always looked downwards as if deep in thought; but he had an ugly expression and cruelty was written in his face. Krusinski adds that his soldiers feared him but admired his great courage.

The circumstance which led to the Afghan invasion are too complicated for discussion here; [91] it must suffice to say that in 1722, after an unsuccessful raid made two years earlier, Mahmud invaded Persia in earnest. Those who believed in portents were little surprised. A disastrous earthquake had recently destroyed the greater part of Tabriz, killing 80,000 people. Then a kind of smog descended upon Isfahan, blotting out the sun and at its setting turning the horizon to blood; and when the Shah went from his capital to Tehran, 'a fiery cloud seemed to surround him' on his arrival there. The court astrologers predicted that blood would soon be shed in Isfahan. For once they were right.

When it became clear that Mahmud was marching on the capital, Husain sent envoys with the offer of a considerable sum of money if he would withdraw with his troops to Afghanistan. This sign of weakness was all that Mahmud needed; he continued his advance to Gulnabad, a village some nine miles from Isfahan. Here, on 8 March 1722, a pitched battle was fought in which 25,000 Afghans routed a Persian army of twice their number and captured a large quantity of booty.

65. Young girl holding a flower. A miniature of the Isfahan school painted c. A. D. 1590. *Treasury, Topkapi Palace Museum, Istanbul.*

153

As refugees began to pour into the city, the inhabitants took the situation to be worse than it actually was. Terrified women rushed screaming through the streets and clamoured to be admitted into the citadel. Yet Isfahan might still have been saved. The Afghan army was small. Help might come from Georgia and elsewhere in the north or west. But Sultan Husain was weak and under the influence of corrupt ministers, some of whom were in enemy pay; every decision that he took was the wrong one.

Sultan Husain had a large family, his three eldest sons being Sultan Mahmud, Safi and Tahmasp—aged twenty-five, twenty-three and eighteen respectively. First Sultan Mahmud was brought out of the harem and appointed the Shah's deputy, with the commission to leave Isfahan and recruit troops in the provinces. Within forty-eight hours he had crossed swords with his father's advisers and was sent back to the harem. Then Safi was summoned to replace him.

Meanwhile Mahmud the Afghan, after some initial hesitation, advanced upon Isfahan and, reaching the Shahristan bridge, pitched camp on the northern bank of the river. For a week he attempted to force an entry into the city from the east, but he could make no headway; he therefore sent a body of men across the river to discover whether Farahabad and Julfa were being defended.

The Siege of Isfahan

Much though the Shah loved his Palace of Farahabad, which was by no means impossible to defend, he had chosen to return to the city. Moreover the Armenians in Julfa had been disarmed for fear that they might go over to the Afghans; Mahmud therefore found that there was nothing to prevent him entering Farahabad, which he made his headquarters, and he took Julfa without bloodshed. There were no executions in Julfa, but an indemnity of 120,000 *tomans* was demanded; this was subsequently reduced to 70,000 *tomans*, which were reluctantly paid. There was also a good deal of looting. About sixty Armenian girls were seized for the harems of Mahmud and his principal officers; but such was the misery of the victims and so loud the wailings of their distracted parents that, very surprisingly, most of the girls were allowed to return to their homes. They were then rebaptized and given to understand by their priests that their ' original purity ' had thus been restored to them.

It was reported that Mahmud's unexpected act of clemency was due to his belief that ' the rape of these girls was the cause of his not yet having taken Isfahan.' He had made more than one attempt to cross the flooded river by the town bridges, but all had ended in failure. The spirits of the Isfahanis rose, and rose still further when they made a successful raid on the Gulnabad battlefield and brought back to Isfahan eighteen of the twenty-four cannons that they had abandoned there after their defeat; but in the main the Persians failed to seize the opportunities that came to them. In particular, an Afghan attack on the Marnan bridge could have been turned into a resounding victory for the Persians if a traitorous general, the *Vali* of Arabistan, had not failed to co-operate. It was everywhere rumoured that the principal concern of the *Vali*, who was drawing fifty *tomans* a day for the duration of the war, was the prolongation of the campaign.

Prince Safi was the best of the Shah's three eldest sons. He was a young man of spirit who, in spite of the handicap of his harem upbringing, had won a clear grasp of the military and political situation. He knew that there were traitors, and that his father still trusted them. He saw that so long as he himself was a mere figurehead, he could do nothing to put an end to corruption. So he went to his

154

68

69

father, denounced the traitors, and said that if he were not given real authority he would return to the harem. Sultan Husain refused; Safi returned to the harem, and was replaced by his youngest brother, Tahmasp.

Tahmasp was feeble, pleasure-loving, and easily led; his appointment was, therefore, popular with the ministers, who saw that they had nothing to fear from a nonentity. But the Isfahanis in general were shrewd enough to realize that Safi's dismissal had been a disaster. Two attempts were made to force Sultan Husain to abdicate in favour of his brother, but they were foiled by the Shah's bodyguard.

Because of their covered galleries, the two major bridges of Isfahan, the Thirty-three-arch bridge and the Khwaju, were almost impregnable. The Persians had always realized that the Marnan bridge, which was farther upstream, was more vulnerable; it was for this reason that they had detailed seasoned Georgian soldiers to guard it. On the night of 6 April Mahmud was informed by his spies that these Georgians, after an orgy, lay in a drunken stupor at their posts. He immediately attacked, and succeeded in establishing a bridge-head on the northern bank of the river. This was the turning-point in the siege.

Though Mahmud had insufficient men to encircle Isfahan, he was able to set up strong-posts and thus make it very difficult for Persian foraging parties to bring supplies back to the town. From now on, little went right for the Persians. A relief force from the north was attacked and routed by the Afghans at Gaz, about nine miles from the city. Another army set out from Georgia, but was recalled. Discontent grew in Isfahan, and there were further unsuccessful attempts to force the Shah to abdicate. Tahmasp, who had left the city with a strong escort to recruit help, only reached Kashan after narrowly avoiding capture by the Afghan patrols under command of Mahmud's cousin, Ashraf. On his arrival, instead of co-operating with the loyal and efficient *Vali* of Luristan, Tahmasp proceeded to Qazvin and was soon immersed in a life of pleasure.

During the first two months of the siege there had been no shortage of food, but in June famine began. Foraging parties, driven to recklessness by hunger, attempted to break through the enemy cordon but were killed almost to a man. Then Mahmud set fire to the cornfields, and a pall of smoke hung for days over the city. Ramadan fell that year in July, but though it brought a temporary lull in the fighting, it brought no comfort to the starving population. Horses, camels and donkeys were eaten first, then cats and dogs.

One day, as I was going from the French to the English Ambassador's palace [wrote Krusinski] seeing a famished woman holding a cat in her hand, which she was desirous of killing, I helped her to slay it, though unwillingly, as her hands were lacerated by its claws, and she was unable to master it.

People who were clad in silk, wrote a Persian historian, now ate leaves like the silk-worm.

Mahmud was also in difficulties, and at the beginning of August he made a peace offer. The terms were harsh; the Shah and his ministers, however, gave them very serious consideration before finally deciding to reject them. It was at this moment that the little village of Ben Isfahan,[92] some five miles to the north-west of the capital, set an example of heroism which, had it been followed by the citizens of Isfahan itself, might yet have saved the day. On 13 August, with the support of refugees from other villages in the neighbourhood, the inhabitants of Ben Isfahan repulsed a strong Afghan attack, killing 300 of the enemy and taking a large number of prisoners including some high-ranking officers. In spite of Mahmud's appeal to the Shah that the lives of these prisoners should be spared, the Ben Isfahanis, who had suffered enough from Afghan brutality, put them all to the sword.

68. Carpet-weaving.
Children are sent to the looms at a very early age.

69. Fruit-seller in the Maidan.

70. Youth drinking.
A mural painting from the period of Abbas II in the Chihil Sutun.

In September cannibalism began in Isfahan. 'For instance (wrote Krusinski) I saw the heads of five butchers laid on a large stone and pounded. They afterwards ate the intestines of the corpses, with which the streets were full'. For bread they ate the leaves and the bark of trees, and the soles of old shoes soaked in water became a luxury dish. Then the women broke out from the seclusion of the *anderun*

... adorned with gems and pearls, clamouring in vain for bread; but no one desired their jewels, or was able to give them food in exchange for them, until they fell at length exhausted and wailing to the earth, and expired. The bodies were cast away unburied, and the river was everywhere full to the brink with them ...[93]

Another eye-witness, the Carmelite Alexander à Sigismundo, confirms Krusinski's report. All the streets and gardens, he wrote, were strewn with piles of rotting corpses. Pieces of flesh, still warm, were cut from the bodies of the newly dead and gobbled down 'without any pepper, with great relish'; youths and girls were enticed into houses to be killed and eaten. 'This sad banquet lasted to October, accompanied by such terrible circumstances that they cannot be described without shedding tears'.[94] But described they are, in detail too gruesome to allow of repetion here.

Krusinski laid much of the blame for these calamities on the folly and improvidence of the Isfahanis. They had missed the opportunity, before Isfahan was completely beseiged, of sending useless mouths out of the city; they had even admitted hordes of starving peasants from the surrounding country, but had laid in no reserves of food. The French ambassador, whose own larder was well stocked, had attempted to reason with the authorities, only to receive the boastful reply, 'Oh! we have sufficient stores to last us for years'.

Meanwhile Mahmud had been waiting for the surrender which he felt sure could not be much longer delayed. Yet even now, at the eleventh hour, there came a sudden ray of hope to the beleaguered: a certain Malik Mahmud, the ambitious Governor of Tun, was reported to be marching with a strong force to relieve the capital. The Afghan leader was alarmed: he saw that the prize might yet be snatched from his outstretched hand. But he acted with his usual energy; by means of handsome gifts as a present reward, and tempting promises for the future, he persuaded the Governor to return to Khurasan and leave Isfahan to its fate.

Mahmud, eager to keep the booty for himself, wanted to spare the city from the plunder of his troops, but it was daily becoming more and more difficult to hold them in check. Yet still the Shah refused to surrender. To pay his troops he had been forced to debase the currency, and to pawn some of the crown jewels to the Dutch and English East India Companies; but in time money ceased to have any value since food could not be bought with it. It was only when the Palace itself began to go hungry that Sultan Husain took desperate action. He then sent an envoy to Mahmud with the offer of 100,000 *tomans*, the provinces of Khurasan and Kerman, and the hand of his daughter in marriage, if he would put an end to the siege. 'Let us make peace', he said, 'and be like father and son'.

But Sultan Husain had left it too late. Mahmud replied haughtily:

The 100,000 *tomans* and the provinces which you offer are already mine; you give me my own money and country, and you also offer me your daughter. What am I to do with your daughter? I shall give all your daughters and all your kin to my slaves. Your suggestion is unreasonable. I shall not take my hands off Isfahan.

After conferring with his ministers, the Shah decided that he had no option: he must abdicate and surrender the city.

71. Late sixteenth-century silk fabric. *Victoria and Albert Museum, London.*

71

The announcement of Sultan Husain's decision was greeted by all his subjects ' with such groans and lamentations that they were heard as far as Julfa and the Afghan camp '. On 22 October the Shah sent his favourite daughter as a gift to Mahmud, and the following day, after having his three remaining camels killed and their flesh distributed among the starving citizens, he rode out with a few of his troops, on horses provided by Mahmud (for all his own had been eaten), to make his submission at the Palace of Farahabad. Among the few who came to see him leave the Palace were the Reverend John Frost, Chaplain to the East India Company, and Mattheus van Leijpzig, the accountant of the Dutch Company; the Isfahanis looked on in silent misery. Crossing the Thirty-three-arch bridge Sultan Husain reached Farahabad where—the final indignity—he was kept waiting for half an hour in the sun until Mahmud, who pretended to be asleep, deigned to receive him.

A detailed account exists written by a man who witnessed all that passed at that fateful interview.[95] Mahmud was seated in one corner of the audience chamber, reclining against a cushion covered with cloth of gold, and the Shah, on entering, was conducted to ' a lower place ' in another corner. Formal greetings having been exchanged, the Shah said, ' My son, since the Supreme Being does not wish me to reign, and the moment has come which he has decreed for you to ascend the throne, I cede my empire to you with all my heart, and I wish that you may rule it in all prosperity '. Then he handed the *jiqa*—the aigrette, set with jewels, that was his badge of royalty—to Amanullah, the Afghan Commander-in-Chief, to give to Mahmud. But Mahmud frowned; the Shah therefore rose and himself placed the *jiqa* on the victor's head.

Refreshments were served, and Mahmud, who could now afford to be magnanimous, made a generous speech in which he promised to look upon the ex-Shah ' as his father ' and to ask his advice on matters of state. Sultan Husain was then taken to rooms that had been made ready for him. ' Thus the Persian empire, which was founded by Ismael, and had lasted 228 years, under nine monarchs, this day ended in Husain, and their annals were finished and closed '.

To prepare for Mahmud's state entry into the capital, Amanullah marched at once with 3000 of his troops to the Maidan and, to the accompaniment of the shrieks and wailing of the women of the ex-Shah's harem, occupied the Palace. Then food was distributed, the streets cleared of corpses, and a deputation of the English East India Company received and assured of favourable treatment that they were not in fact to receive.

Every precaution was taken to prevent disturbances when, several days later, the new Shah entered Isfahan, but the population had neither strength nor spirit—not even, it seems, the desire—to make a hostile demonstration. Several eye-witnesses have described in detail the splendid cortège, led by twelve heralds and 2000 Afghan cavalry, which set out from Farahabad for the city. The wretched Sultan Husain rode on the left of the conqueror. There were 300 Negroes, dressed in scarlet cloth. There were camels carrying harquebuses, and a large band. After the procession had crossed the Khwaju Bridge, Sultan Husain was conducted by way of a back street to the Palace of his confinement while Mahmud continued his triumphal progress. The cannons roared, the band played; and the townsfolk, believing that the future could not have worse in store for them than the past, laid aside their grief and strewed the way with carpets and brocades. Then, to cries of ' Allah! ' from the soldiers, Shah Mahmud entered the Palace gates. The short-lived Afghan rule had begun.

72. Book cover
(early seventeenth century).
Victoria and Albert Museum, London.

163

Mahmud Shah's appearance has already been described; Father Krusinski completes the picture by adding to it an account of his character and his daily routine. Though in appearance as unregal as Sultan Husain, in every other respect Mahmud was the antithesis of his feeble, pious and drunken predecessor:

> Every morning he exercised himself in wrestling half an hour with some of the most robust of his officers, and spent the rest of the day in other exercises proper to harden and strengthen his body. Five sheep were brought him daily with their feet tied, for him to cut them in two with his sabre. He was very dexterous in flinging a little javelin, called *girid* in Persia, and never failed of striking the mark he aimed at. He was so nimble in mounting his horse, that without a stirrup, he would lay hold of the horse's mane with his left hand, and clapping his right on his back, would leap into the saddle. He slept very little, and never made use of mattresses in a campaign. He went the rounds himself, accompanied by some of his most trusty friends, to visit the sentinels in the night; not only in the camp, but in Isfahan itself. He was very sober in his diet and drink, contenting himself with what he found: and as an effect of his sobriety, he was so exactly continent, that he never had commerce with any woman but his wife, Shah Husain's daughter, by whom he had a son ...[96]

The new reign began well. Mahmud brought large supplies of food into the city. He also made himself popular by ordering the execution of those Persians in high office who had betrayed their country, saying that such men might in turn have betrayed him; only the Vali of Arabistan was spared death—possibly because he was, like Mahmud, a Sunni. Moreover the Shah, realizing that the government of a civilized and highly developed, if decadent, nation was for the present beyond the powers of rough Afghan tribesmen, retained Persian ministers in office; but to each he attached an Afghan who was to act as an understudy and prevent intrigue and corruption.

Sultan Husain was kept in confinement and his harem reduced to his legitimate wives, his concubines being distributed among Mahmud's officials. The princes too, with the exception of Tahmasp who was safely out of reach, were imprisoned, though for them this involved no more than a change of gaoler. The royal treasury, or what remained of it, was seized and the possessions of those Isfahanis who had died during the siege or in battle were confiscated. The citizens of both Isfahan and Julfa were also heavily taxed, but after defeat in war this was looked upon as inevitable; the people grumbled but they paid.

Mahmud's position, however, was far from secure. Admittedly he had taken the capital and forced the Shah to abdicate, and soon he was also master of Qum, Kashan and Qazvin; but he still controlled only a part of Persia. He knew that the Persians despised the Afghans as barbarians and hated them for being Sunnis. His troubles increased when Tahmasp had himself proclaimed Shah in Qazvin, and when the Russians, announcing that they would restore the Safavid dynasty, invaded Persia from the north. Then the Turks, taking advantage of the general chaos, invaded Georgia and occupied large territories in western Persia.

Had Tahmasp behaved like a man at this juncture, he might yet have marched on Isfahan and driven out the Afghans, but he was hopeless: the worse the news, the more he drank; and after the fall of Isfahan he was only intermittently sober. The ministers and courtiers who then surrounded him merely encouraged his orgies and themselves took part in them. When Mahmud sent Amanullah to attack him, Tahmasp fled to Tabriz.

Qazvin, finding itself deserted, surrendered. But the Afghan Commander's extortions and brutalities were soon such that, two months later, on 8 January 1723, the Qazvinis rose to a man and ejected the Afghans with heavy loss. In Isfahan Mahmud heard the news with dismay. Fearing lest this successful uprising would lead to a revolt in the capital, he announced that his commander had decisively defeated Tahmasp in battle and had taken him prisoner. The compulsory public rejoicings and illuminations ordered in celebration of the alleged victory were swiftly succeeded by the entry into Isfahan of the bedraggled remnants of Amanullah's army. Mahmud, his trick exposed, saw that the situation was now more critical than before. He decided upon prompt and ruthless action.

Orders were given for the principal Persian ministers and nobles to attend, that same evening, at the Palace to discuss the terms of a peace treaty with Tahmasp. They came, suspecting nothing, but only one man [97] left the Palace alive: the rest

Fig. 21. View of the Maidan (from *La Perse*, by Mme Dieulafoy, 1887).

were butchered on the spot. A Dutch friar, who was with his compatriots in the garden of the Dutch Factory half a mile away, recorded that they heard

> ... a frightful tumult and pitiful screaming ... We were nearly dumb, not knowing what it meant, although such screams had sometimes been heard at night, as the Afghans now and then broke into people's houses, and murdered them. The next morning the murdered grandees and King's slaves were laid out naked on their backs in the forecourt of the palace, so that everyone could see what bloody revenge the tyrant Mahmud had taken.[98]

Several hundred people were killed in this first massacre. Next it was the turn of their sons—' about 200 young gentlemen ... bred up in a college to acquire learning and the knowledge of military exercises '. These were taken out into the country, released, and told to run for their lives. Then they were hunted like hares and shot down. Finally 300 of the Qizilbash Guards were also slaughtered.

Mahmud's brutality achieved its object. The Isfahanis, struck dumb with terror, hardly dared to leave their houses. The city gates were closely guarded, and shut even against those who were bringing supplies of food to the capital. Famine returned.

During the next two years Mahmud and his commanders were busy attempting to subdue the rest of Persia. Sometimes they were victorious, sometimes ignominiously defeated. Shiraz, after a heroic stand, was finally starved into submission. Before Yazd, so important for the security of his communications with Kandahar, Mahmud was completely routed and only just escaped with his life.

The defeat outside Yazd, which the army blamed upon Mahmud, brought the troops to the verge of mutiny. They had long been clamouring to return home to their families, or that their families might be brought to Isfahan; some attempt had been made to carry out the latter project, but the journey through enemy-held territory remained precarious. Amongst those who came from Kandahar was Mahmud's mother, who

> ... arrived at Isfahan, mounted on a camel which, except scarlet housing, had nothing to distinguish it from the rest. She had no women, no officers, no servants with her when she crossed the Maidan, and came to the principal gate of the new King's Palace half naked, and what clothes she had all in tatters, ravenously gnawing a great radish she held in her hand, more like a witch than the mother of a great King.

The troops also demanded the recall from Kandahar of Mahmud's capable and popular cousin, Ashraf, who had fallen into disgrace after letting Tahmasp escape from Isfahan during the siege. Mahmud reluctantly agreed: between himself and Ashraf, whose father he had murdered, there had never been any love lost. Mahmud had also, some time before this, quarrelled with his Commander-in-Chief, Amanullah. He found himself with two very dangerous enemies.

Mahmud, who by now was in a highly neurotic state, decided to go into a 'retreat'—to make what Malcolm described as 'Tapassa, or abstraction of the soul from the contemplation of all sublunary objects till he becomes absorbed in the Divinity.'[99] After incarcerating himself in a vault for forty days with no company and only bread and water for sustenance, he emerged in a state of nervous depression that bordered upon insanity.

It was while he was in this condition that he was informed that Safi, Sultan Husain's eldest son, had escaped from the harem. Though the report was almost certainly untrue, Mahmud seized this pretext to exterminate the former royal family. On the afternoon of 7 February 1725, all the remaining princes of the blood royal, including three decrepit old uncles of Sultan Husain, were summoned to the courtyard of the Palace. And here they were butchered to death by Mahmud himself and two of his guards; only Sultan Husain and two small children were spared.

After this gruesome massacre Mahmud's mind broke down completely, although he still had occasional brief interludes of relative lucidity. The Afghan doctors, having failed to improve his condition, took the curious step of summoning the Armenian clergy to recite a part of the Red Gospel[100] over him—a procedure which was at that time a fashionable treatment for insanity among the Isfahanis. The clergy came to the Palace in solemn procession, wearing their priestly robes and bearing lighted candles in their hands. They were received with great respect, and after the ceremony were escorted back to Julfa by a number of court officials.

It so happened that Mahmud had a lucid interval soon after the priests had left him. To mark his gratitude, he sent a very handsome present to the Armenians, and also repaid the English and Dutch East India Companies some of the money that he had previously appropriated. It may be mentioned here that Mahmud's successor was in due course to reclaim these contributions on the excuse that they had been made by a man whose brain was disordered at the time.

73. A woman drinking wine. A miniature of the Isfahan school, c. A.D. 1650. *Treasury, Topkapi Palace Museum. Istanbul.*

73

Soon, however, Mahmud's condition became critical. Some said that he suffered from palsy, others from leprosy; and one author suggests a form of elephantiasis. ' One half of his body rotted ', writes Krusinski—and he adds revolting details. Then Mahmud became delirious, ' and in the horrid torments he endured, he turned his fury against himself, and tore his hands with his teeth.' [101] It was at this juncture that troops of the drunken Tahmasp defeated an Afghan contingent at Qum. With Mahmud incapable of ruling, drastic action had to be taken. His elder brother was his obvious successor; but he was in Kandahar, and time was short. Therefore Amanullah freed the imprisoned Ashraf and together they marched on Isfahan. Reaching the Maidan, they overpowered the guard and entered the Palace. Three days later Mahmud was dead—due to his illness or at the hands of Ashraf—nobody can be sure. On 26 April 1725 Ashraf was proclaimed Shah.

So perished Mahmud, at the early age of twenty-six. His career had been remarkable. Chingiz Khan and Tamerlane had conquered with great armies; Mahmud had captured Isfahan and half Persia with 20,000 wild tribesmen. But of his reign, wrote Sykes,

> ... with the exception of the first few months of just rule after the capitulation of Isfahan, little good can be said. He was treacherous, narrow-minded, lacking in generosity and indeed in almost all the qualities which stamp a great conqueror; on the other hand, he was brave and energetic. Like Afghans in general, he was entirely deficient in administrative qualities and his mind was quite uncultivated. Finally, the massacres for which he was responsible have consigned his memory to wholly justifiable execration.[102]

ASHRAF SHAH (1725-29)

Ashraf, who was probably about the same age as his cousin, was experienced and capable, shrewd, and popular with his soldiers. His reign began with the now familiar wholesale slaughter of all who might stand in his way—that is to say, of almost everyone who had held positions of authority under Mahmud. Among those killed was his dangerous rival, Amanullah. By this and other cunning acts he initially made a good impression on the Isfahanis. He gathered up the remains of the murdered Safavid princes, which still lay rotting in the Palace yard, and sent them with much pomp and many expressions of pretended sympathy to be interred in the royal mausoleum at Qum. He even went so far as to make a token offer of the crown to Sultan Husain, who very sensibly declined it. He took as his wife one of the daughters of the ex-Shah, quadrupled his allowance, and allowed the old man to amuse himself by putting him in charge of all the building operations in the palace grounds. ' The buildings were likely to be the more perfect for it ', wrote Krusinski, ' since nobody understood that art or had a better taste for it, than Shah Husain, who, indeed, hardly understood anything else.' [103]

The story now becomes very confused,[104] but the fact of prime importance is the emergence of a certain Nadir Kuli, destined, as Nadir Shah, to be the last great Asiatic conqueror.

Nadir, who had been born and bred in Khurasan, was a natural leader of men, and he dreamed of conquest. Of humble stock, he had graduated by way of brigandry to becoming the commander of his own army. Still far too weak to attack Ashraf, he turned his attention to the more immediate problem of the attitude that he should adopt towards ' Shah ' Tahmasp, who had managed to rally those Persians hoping to restore the Safavid dynasty. First he attacked Tahmasp but failed to take him prisoner; then he changed his strategy and decided to throw in his lot with him for as long as it suited his purposes. In November 1726 he wrested Meshed from Malik Mahmud. He was at this time about thirty-eight years old.

74. Carpet
(early seventeenth century).
Tehran National Museum.

75. Carpet. *Tehran National Museum.*

Soon, however, there was rivalry between Nadir and Tahmasp. The contrast between the two men could hardly have been greater. Avramov, Tahmasp's Russian interpreter, has sketched [105] a brilliant portrait of the young Prince—of his passion for vodka and his methods of getting hold of it; of his swift changes of mood, from ferocity to gaiety and back again, when under its influence; and of his fondness for salacious stories. Avramov makes it clear he was no fool; but he was weak-willed and debauched. Nadir, on the other hand, was forceful, ambitious, full of self-confidence, and of inexhaustible energy. He was no puritan, but he never let his pleasures interfere with his dreams of conquest and power. Nadir for the time-being was making use of Tahmasp's prestige as the legitimate heir to the Persian throne (there were some seventeen other pretenders at this time); when he had squeezed the lemon dry, it would be easy enough to throw it away.

After two years of victories and defeats, plots and counterplots, Nadir felt himself strong enough to challenge Ashraf. The decisive battle took place in November 1729 at Murchakhur, about thirty-five miles to the north of the capital. The Afghans fought well, but after the loss of 4000 men their courage broke and they fled to Isfahan. Next morning before dawn a huge caravan left Isfahan for Shiraz: Ashraf had abandoned the capital. His last act there had been to murder the aged and harmless Sultan Husain.[106]

Nadir and his army entered Isfahan on 13 November; Tahmasp, who had been kept out of the way so as not to diminish Nadir's glory, was allowed to join him there three weeks later. More than seven years had passed since he had made his escape through the Afghan lines to Tabriz, and though he was warmly received by the Isfahanis, he is said to have wept when he saw the decay and desolation all around him. But in the Palace a pleasurable surprise awaited him. When he entered the harem, an old woman threw her arms about his neck in great transports of joy. It was his mother who, ever since the invasion of the Afghans, had lived on in the Palace disguised as a slave.

Tahmasp was crowned again; but it was Nadir who ruled. In December Nadir marched on Shiraz and captured the town. Ashraf managed to make his escape, bue his time was running out. Although the exact circustances of his death are not known for certain, it would appear that he was involved in a skirmish and shot through the head in a running fight somewhere in the south-west of Persia. His head, together with a large diamond that he had with him, was sent to Shah Tahmasp II.

> Thus the Afghans were drowned in a torrent of blood [wrote Sykes]. They had achieved a remarkable conquest with slender means, and, had their fellow-tribesmen joined them in sufficient numbers, they might have held their own for some time against a national revival. But their barbarous organization, while good enough for conquest, massacre, and destruction, was totally incapable of administering the kingdom they had won so easily. The invaders remained, therefore, a numerically small band of hated aliens, which, even under a fine leader like Ashraf, could not stand against the troops of Nadir.[107]

SHAH TAHMASP II (1729-32), SHAH ABBAS III (1732-36)

Nadir's services to Persia, in driving out the Afghans, were such as to merit, indeed to necessitate, a substantial reward. As a youth he had dreamed that he had caught a fish with four horns, and this he had interpreted as meaning that he would conquer four kingdoms; for the moment, however, he had to be content with the gift of four provinces—Khurasan, Sistan, Kerman and Mazandaran. Tahmasp even offered him the title of Sultan; but Nadir refused. It was better to wait for the throne.

Having disposed of the Afghans, Nadir now challenged the Turks and in a successful campaign recovered Irak and Azarbaijan; then he was forced to turn east to quell a rebellion in Khurasan. At this point Tahmasp, perhaps a little

76. Young Isfahani girl.

77

78

Fig. 22. Persian Dress in the 18th Century (from *Travels*, by C. de Bruyn, 1737).

jealous of Nadir's successes, and perhaps a little sobered by the realization that he had become no more than a figure-head, decided to take the field in person against the Turks. The result was disastrous: within a short space of time he had lost all the territory that Nadir had so recently recovered. The treaty that Tahmasp subsequently signed with the Sultan gave Nadir the opening for which he had been waiting: he marched upon Isfahan to overthrow Tahmasp.

After ceremonial visits had been exchanged between Tahmasp and Nadir, the latter invited the Shah to a 'reception' in the Hazarjarib garden. The reception became an orgy which continued for three days and nights. Then Nadir, who had doubtless planned the matter carefully in advance, displayed to the citizens of Isfagan the 'sot and sodomite' who was their theoretical ruler, whereupon there was, we are told, general agreement that he should be deposed. He was immediately carried away and imprisoned. This was in 1732, and the puppet Shah had reigned for less than three years.

Nadir still considered that the time was not yet ripe for him to assume the throne and, for this reason, resorted to the age-old device of appointing an infant—the Shah's eight-month-old son, Abbas—Shah of Persia. During the next four years Nadir won victory after victory over the Turks, and obliged the Russians to evacuate the Caspian provinces that they had been occupying. His prestige thus became such that he could safely depose the infant Abbas III. The child was sent to join his father in prison in Khurasan, where four years later they were both murdered.

At a moment proclaimed as auspicious by the court astrologers—namely on 8 March 1736, 'at eight hours and twenty minutes after sunrise'—Nadir Quli, after an unconvincing show of reluctance, allowed himself to be crowned Shah of Persia. With his transference of the capital to Meshed, Isfahan now became once again, and has remained ever since, a provincial city.

77. Astrolabe. Isfahan work, dated A. D. 1712.

78. Box or possibly cartridge case of cut steel, signed Hajii Abbas and probably Isfahan work c. A. D. 1700.

Nadir Shah's career as a conqueror was amazing.[108] Within four years he had taken Delhi, Bokhara and Khiva. He had completed the recovery of the territory seized by the Turks. He had extended the Persian empire until it stretched from the Oxus in the north to the Indus in the south—so constituting a realm far greater than that ruled over by Abbas the Great. This was the climax of his career: the seven years that remained to him saw an ever-increasing ruthlessness and brutality which finally reached a pitch that is only explicable on the assumption that he was insane. He was, indeed, as has been said of him, the very apt pupil of Chingiz Khan and of Tamerlane.

Nadir Shah was not often in Isfahan, but two visits that he paid to the former capital were long remembered by its inhabitants. On the first occasion he arrived on 28 December 1745 and remained for about five weeks. As one of the Carmelite Friars observed:

> It was the day of the Holy Innocents, and indeed that second Herod, more cruel than the first, ... on the very day of his entry at once opened the courts of his injustice, in which he alone sat as accuser, witness and judge, avarice serving as his counsel, tyranny as his authorities, his own arbitrary will as the law. He immediately began the horrible butchery by having slaughtered under various pretexts a quantity of the chief persons of the country, among the principal of whom were the Governor of Isfahan and the mayor of Julfa ... It was a sight to see in all parts of the city, and especially in the great Maidan, numbers of people of every grade tortured by the royal officials in order to extract money from them in accordance with the orders of the tyrant. To cut off noses and ears, put out eyes, mutilate members, make all the toe-nails drop off under blows of the bastinado—these were ordinary affairs, from which the more prominent personages of the Court and even the chief officers of the royal army were not exempt ... So it began and so it continued until his departure from Isfahan for Meshed ...[109]

Nadir, on leaving, gave orders that the Armenians were to collect a considerable sum of money, which was to be paid within the space of a few months. Not surprisingly, all those Armenians who could afford it made their escape to Basra, Baghdad or elsewhere with their wives and families before Nadir's return to Isfahan at the end of 1746.

By that time his avarice and homicidal mania had reached such a pitch that he must be considered as no longer responsible for his actions. For the bastinado, red-hot iron bars now replaced the traditional sticks and usually resulted in death. Parents unable to bear the torture, sold their sons and daughters for a few pence to become the instruments of pleasure of the soldiery. Men were burnt alive in the Maidan; men were buried alive ... In the course of a few weeks, and at the cost of some 5000 persons murdered or maimed for life, the Shah had managed to squeeze 300,000 *tomans* from a populace that had seemed to have been bled dry a year before. And elsewhere in Persia it was the same story, or worse: there were the towers of skulls, the basketfuls of eyes ...

But the end was in sight. Five months later Nadir was assassinated by the captain of his guards, when he was marching to quell a revolt in Kuchan. He was fifty-nine years old.

Nadir was described, by one who saw him towards the end of his life,[120] as being tall and handsome—' one of the most comely men I ever beheld. The injury the sun and weather have done to his complexion only gives him a more manly aspect.' His beard was full and black, his voice so stentorian that in battle it terrified his enemies. There seems little doubt that the deterioration of his character was largely due to the breakdown of his health, though Lord Byron, who calls him ' that costive Sophy,' seems to be going rather far in making chronic constipation the principal cause of his mad outbursts of sadism. His Jesuit doctor, whose account was no doubt

79. Shah Abbas the Great. An Indian miniature by Bishn Das. Photo: *British Museum, London.*

80. Tower of skulls. This particular one only shows trophies of the chase. From *Voyages* by Sir J. Chardin, 1723. Photo: *British Museum, London.*

81. A view of the Maidan showing the square used as a market. From *Travels* by C. de Bruyn, 1737. Photo: *British Museum, London.*

82. Entrance to the Royal Bazaar. In the distance is the Royal Mosque. From *Voyage en Perse* by E. Flandin and P. Coste, 1851. Photo: *British Museum, London.*

83. The Chahar Bagh as it appeared in the nineteenth century. From *Voyage en Perse* by E. Flandin and P. Coste, 1851. Photo: *British Museum, London.*

79

81

83

> ... was slain, the sinner!
> Because he could no more digest his dinner.[111]

Nadir was more or less unlettered, yet he gave a large collection of manuscripts to the Library of the Shrine at Meshed. He erected many buildings—but not in Isfahan which, when it ceased to be the capital, concerned him but little. He was a brilliant commander and an inspired organizer, who by sheer force of personality built up an efficient army out of most unpromising material. War was his greatest pleasure in life (and next to war, he once said, a good melon and a good horse). Religion did not interest him, and his restoration of the Sunni doctrine was a purely political gesture. One day, in discussion with a *mulla*, he was shocked to learn that there would be no war in Paradise; 'Then how,' he asked, 'can there be any delights there?'..

ANARCHY (1747-87)

With the murder of the tyrant there came no respite for his wretched subjects. Nadir hwah had ruled brutally—but at least he had ruled. For the next forty years, civil hars and chaos, bloodshed and treachery, were only interrupted by the wise and humane government of Karim Khan, a member of the Zand tribe, who set himself up as *Vakil*, or Regent, in Shiraz. Karim Khan died in 1779, in his eightieth year, having been the virtual ruler of Persia for nearly twenty years.

After Karim Khan's death came a further period of civil war, the three main contestants for power being the descendants of Nadir Shah, the Zands, and the Qajars—a Turkish tribe who had been settled in Armenia since the days of Tamerlane. In 1787 the Qajar leader, the eunuch Agha Muhammad, emerged as victor and was proclaimed Shah, and seven years later his last remaining rival, the handsome and brave young Zand chief, Lutfali Khan, was taken prisoner and put to death. The Qajar dynasty, which had Tehran as its capital, remained in power until 1925.

Throughout these bitter years of internecine strife, Isfahan was twice looted—first by the Bakhtiari tribesmen and later by rebel Afghans and Lurs. The proud city, which in the seventeenth century had been as large as London, had, by the close of the eighteenth century, become a wilderness.

THE FATE OF THE CHRISTIANS

Throughout the troubled years of the eighteenth century the Christians in Isfahan and Julfa fared badly.

During the siege of Isfahan, the English and Dutch Companies both hired soldiers, Armenians or Europeans, to defend their factories. They both, unlike the Persian authorities, laid in supplies in good time, and both refused to give Sultan Husain military assistance. But finally, after much protesting, they were obliged to help the Shah financially. The Europeans suffered many indignities, but the only loss of life sustained was of two English factors who attempted to escape from Isfahan and were never heard of again.

Under the Afghans, trade came virtually to a standstill. The Companies were bullied and browbeaten in an attempt to extort money. The Dutch suffered a good

84. Palace of Mirrors.
Now destroyed, this palace
once stood on the bank of the river.
From *Monuments Modernes
de la Perse* by P. Soste, 1867.
Photo: *British Museum, London.*

85. Entrance to the Royal Mosque.
On the left is the Lutfullah Mosque.
From *Voyage en Perse*
by E. Flandin and P. Coste, 1851
Photo: *British Museum London.*

Fig. 23. Armenian Women at Julfa (from *La Perse*, by Mme Dieulafoy, 1887).

deal at the hands of Mahmud's mace-bearer, a ' beastly tyrant ' named Muhammad Nishan, who threatened the bastinado and even decapitation if the money was not paid over; ' We shall see,' he said, ' how the cudgels shall dance on the Dutch backs.' But although the Dutch did eventually pay a total of some 23,000 *tomans* —a considerable sum—their factory was later looted and the factors maltreated.

The English were persecuted by Amanullah, the Afghan Commander-in-Chief, described by the chief factor, a man named Phillipps, as ' a villain of the first magnitude ', who carried away royal jewels that had been deposited at the factory by the ex-Shah as security for a loan. But they were not actually manhandled.

The advent of Ashraf in 1725 made at first little difference to the Companies. Admittedly he began by demanding money from the English, but he soon came to realize that they had none to give. Four years later, however, Ashraf, after beng defeated by Nadir in battle, retreated to Isfahan where he stripped and imprisoned the English factors to prevent them attempting to make common cause with the Persians. Very probably the same happened to the Dutch, whose factory was again ransacked. Seventeen days later, when Ashraf fled to Shiraz, the English bribed their gaolers and were set free; they had been more fortunate than their colleagues in Shiraz, whose chief had been flogged.

With the transference of the capital to Meshed the Isfahan factories were closed down, and such trade as was carried on in the turbulent days that followed was directed from stations on the Gulf.

The Armenians in Julfa were vigorously persecuted by Nadir Shah, who quite unjustly accused them of complicity with the Afghans during the siege of Isfahan. He forbade Christian worship, extorted savage penalties and taxes, and imposed social ostracism. The town steadily dwindled. On the death of the Shah in 1747, more of its wretched inhabitants fled to Georgia, to India and to Baghdad. By the beginning of the nineteenth century the population had shrunk to two or three thousand, and even towards the end of the century it was little larger. Today, in spite of the restoration of religious freedom, the population is probably no more than 10,000, of whom perhaps half are Armenians.

The missionaries were no less unfortunate. At the time of the siege the Carmelites moved out of Isfahan to Julfa, and by 1724 community life in the convent had come to an end; it was then occupied only by one Lay Brother and a servant, who earned their living by gardening and keeping hens. Bishop Philip Mary seems to have been the last Carmelite in sacerdotal orders to inhabit the convent, where he died in 1749; but a Lay Brother remained until 1754.

In the same year Father Sebastian, Bishop of Isfahan but established in the relative safety of Basra, wrote to Rome expressing his hope that

> ... those few Christians who remain in Julfa along with four Religious and missionaries—one of my Order [Carmelite], another a Dominican, another a Jesuit, besides a good [Armenian] priest——may also be able to escape from a country which at present has become so evil and so dangerous both for the soul and for the body, a country I can truly say where iniquity is at present at its height, a country of hell. Poor Persia! [113]

Three years later the Carmelite Convent was seized and taken over by a Persian.

By 1765 there was not in Isfahan itself ' one single baptized soul, Catholic or Armenian ', and only a handful in Julfa and these mostly women. The Carmelite convent is known to have been still standing in 1810, but, like those of the Augustinians and the Capuchins, it remained in the hands of the infidels. It was not until forty years later that Roman Catholic missionaries (this time Lazarists) returned to undertake the thankless work of converting Muslims to Christianity.

Part 4   The nineteenth century

THE QAJARS

THE BRUTAL AGHA MUHAMMAD, who was proclaimed Shah in 1787, was perhaps the most hated of all Iranian monarchs. Soon after his accession he made Tehran his capital, and Isfahan was little troubled by him. Ten years later he was murdered by his personal attendants.

Three other Qajars ruled between them for almost the whole of the nineteenth century: Fath Ali Shah (1798-1834), Muhammad (1834-48) and Nasir ad-din (1848-96). Isfahan was little involved in the political troubles and international disputes of their reigns. Slowly, almost in spite of herself, Iran emerged from a medieval into the semblance of a modern state which aroused the cupidity of the European powers; that she managed to retain her independence was more the result of European rivalries than of her own skill or strength. At the close of the century the Qajar house was still standing; but its walls were cracking and its foundations in very poor repair.

VISITORS TO ISFAHAN

With his habitual thoroughness, Lord Curzon has listed the principal travellers who visited and wrote about Persia in the nineteenth century, down to the year 1891 when he himself was busy co-ordinating the notes of his own recent visit there. He mentions no less than 198 persons; and though Isfahan was at this time no longer the capital, the large majority of these very naturally made a point of seeing the city which had been so famous under the Safavids and which, even in its decay, still mirrored the glory of its great past.

Among those mentioned by Curzon are Sir John Malcolm, James Morier, Sir Robert Ker Porter, Charles Texier, Eugène Flandin, X-P Coste, Dr C. J. Wills and Jane Dieulafoy. Last, but very far from least, there is of course Lord Curzon himself.

JAMES MORIER

James Morier had been brought up in Constantinople, where his father was consul-general to the Levant Company; he was therefore familiar from childhood with Orientals and their ways, and on his entering the diplomatic service it was natural that he should have been chosen to accompany several embassies to Persia. The first was that of Sir Harford Jones in 1808, the second that of Sir Gore Ouseley in 1811. Morier's accounts of these two journeys, valuable though they are, have been eclipsed in popularity by his immortal picaresque novel, *The Adventures of Hajji Baba of Ispahan* (1824), which gives an unsurpassed impression of the Persian character. He also wrote a number of other novels dealing with Persia, but none is comparable to *Hajji Baba* in merit.

86

87

89

90

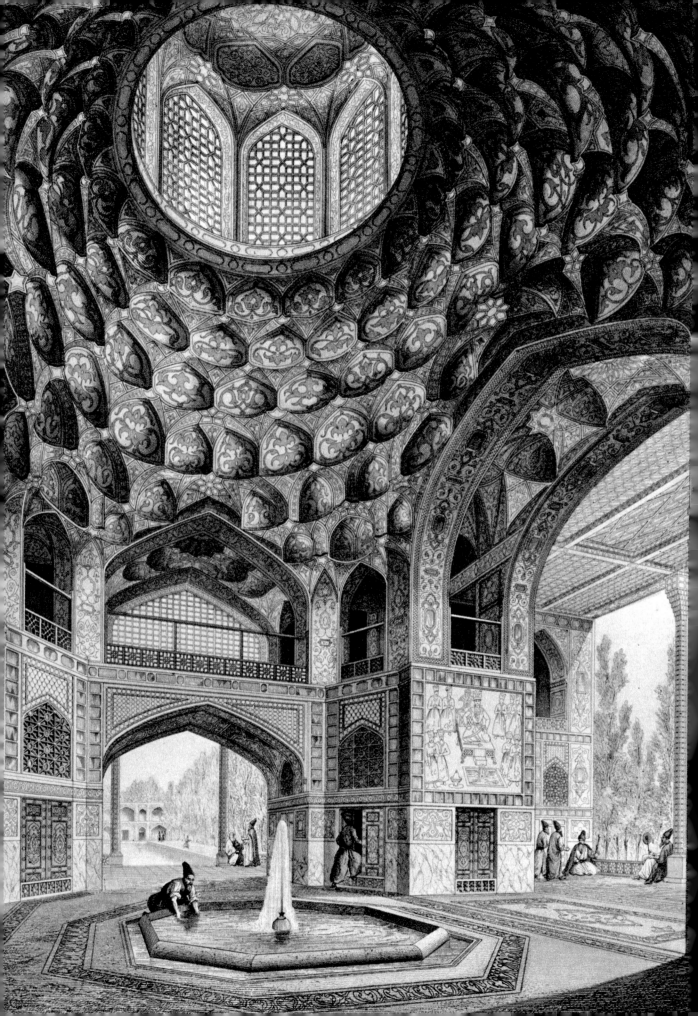

Morier, especially in the account of his second journey to Persia, has left a good description of Isfahan as it appeared in the early years of the nineteenth century. From a distance at which ruins were indistinguishable from habitable houses, the city still gave the impression of considerable size; a closer view, however, showed that about three-quarters of the buildings were in fact no more than shells. But the new Governor, the Amin ed-Dowleh, who had started life as a greengrocer, had already begun to rebuild. The Chahar Bagh and one or two neighbouring avenues had been replanted, though Morier dismissed the result as 'pure vanity'—an attempt to distract attention from the decay on every hand:

> One might suppose that God's curse had extended over parts of this city, as it did over Babylon [Morier wrote]. Houses, bazaars, mosques, palaces, whole streets, are to be seen in total abandonment; and I have rode for miles among its ruins, without meeting with any living creature, except perhaps a jackal peeping over a wall, or a fox running to his hole.[114]

Morier was struck by the mean exteriors of the houses, which were mostly of one storey only.

> A poor man's door is scarcely three feet in height; and this is a precautionary measure to hinder the servants of the great from entering it on horseback, which, when any act of oppression is going on, they would make no scruple to do. But the habitation of a great man in power is known by his gate, which is generally elevated in proportion to the vanity of the owner.[115]

He loved to wander through the bazaars, with their scenes that constantly recalled the Arabian Nights:

> The young Christian merchant; the lady of quality riding on a mule, attended by her eunuch and her she-slave; the Jewish physician; the *dalal*, or crier, showing goods about; the barber Alnascar, sitting with his back against the wall in a very little shop, and thus almost every character may be met with. The Mollahs, or men of the law, are generally to be seen riding about on mules; and they also count it a dignity, and suited to their character, to ride on *white asses*, which is a striking illustration of what we read in Judges v. 10. *Speak ye that ride on white asses, ye that sit in judgement.*[116]

In the company of the Royal Gardener, Morier visited the Shaking Minarets— which, it would appear, had already become a show-piece for visitors—and was duly astonished by the demonstration. He attended, with the ambassador, a reception given by the Governor, who had secured some European-style chairs for the occasion. These were of various heights, and the unfortunate Persian guests were much perplexed as to how to manage their food. 'Some were seated upon chairs so high that they towered far above the alpine scenery of meats and stews; others again were seated so low that they were lost in the valleys, their mouths being brought to about the level of the table.'[117]

After the meal the guests were conducted through dark and intricate avenues to the *divankhaneh*, or reception hall, which was illuminated by wall lamps and tallow candles hung on wires. 'The blaze was immense', wrote Morier, 'and the stench in proportion'. The party wound up with the customary display of fireworks.

The ambassador and his suite were lodged at Saadatabad, on the outskirts of Julfa. Of Julfa Morier wrote that it was in an even more deplorable state than Isfahan itself, though there were houses still standing which spoke eloquently of its former wealth. A single missionary remained—an Italian Dominican named Father Yusuf, who in fifteen years' residence had acquired hardly a word of Persian. He did, however, speak Turkish and Armenian; but he talked with Morier in Italian, and the latter found it a great joy to meet a resident who spoke a European language. Father Yusuf lived alone with his cat, carefully tending his handsome church and his flock of fifteen souls. Although pitifully poor, he firmly and honourably refused to sell to Morier a number of books and manuscripts from the church library which had taken the Englishman's fancy.

91. The Pleasure Pavilion of the Hasht Bihisht (or Eight Paradises). From *Monuments Modernes de la Perse* by P. Coste, 1867. Photo: *British Museum, London.*

In the company of the embassy surgeon, Morier also visited the convent of Armenian nuns, 'nine in number, all old except two, and all ugly.' Having dispensed medicines, the Englishmen went on to the house of an Armenian priest who had asked for treatment for his family. For the mother, suffering from a cataract which she would not allow him to 'couch,' he could do nothing. Nor was there much to be done for the wife—'a jolly young dame' who, in order to get a sight of the foreigners, alleged a sharp attack of 'heart-ache.'

There was a good deal of sickness in Isfahan and Julfa at the time. The Isfahanis were fond of praising their climate, but Morier considered that the city was extremely unhealthy in the summer; most of the embassy staff became ill, and one of them died. Morier was not sorry when news came that the Shah was returning to his capital and the embassy received orders to meet him there.

French Archaeologists

Several French expeditions to Persia, made during the nineteenth century and supported by ample funds, resulted in the production of sumptuous and finely illustrated volumes. Charles Texier, architect and archaeologist, went to Persia in 1839 and on his return published his *Description de l'Arménie, de la Perse ...* (1842-5). Xavier-Pascal Coste, a Marseillais, accompanied a French embassy to Persia in 1840; he was later associated with Eugène Flandin, artist and archaeologist, and the two men, working sometimes together and sometimes independently, produced a number of books. Marcel Dieulafoy and his intrepid wife, Jane, excavated at Susa between 1881 and 1886 and sent back superb antiquities to the Louvre. Mme Dieulafoy's *La Perse ...* (1886) describes their travels and adventures. By far and away the best illustrations of Isfahan as it appeared before restoration and 'tidying-up' began in the thirties of the present century are to be found in these French books, some of the plates of which are reproduced in this present volume.

Lord Curzon

No previous work on Persia had ever approached, nor has any subsequent one surpassed, Lord Curzon's monumental *Persia and the Persian Question* (1892). It is almost incredible that a young man, as the result of only six months' travel in the country, could have produced this astonishing corpus of material which covers every aspect of the country—its history, geography, architecture, politics, customs and communications. This inexhaustible mine has been worked by every subsequent author on Persia, and the very high price that a second-hand copy of it still commands is ample evidence of its value even after the lapse of more than seventy years.[118]

The Zil

Next in importance in Iran to Nasir ad-din Shah, during much of his long reign, was his son Sultan Mas'ud Mirza, known as the Zil-es-Sultan or 'Shadow of the King'; the name was inappropriate: like several of his brothers he was double his father's size.

Under the Safavid Shahs, any one of the royal children might be appointed heir; but the Qajars had reverted to the old Tartar or Turkish custom of the right of primogeniture—provided always that the mother of the prince was of royal origin. The Zil-es-Sultan was the eldest of Nasir ad-din's surviving sons,[119] but his mother was of plebeian atock and he had been passed over in favour of the next brother, Muzaffir-ad-Din, who was proclaimed *Vali-Ahd*, or Heir Apparent. When he was a mere boy, however, the Zil had been made Governor of Isfahan, then of Shiraz also; and finally so much power was given to him that from his palace in Isfahan he ruled over little less than half of Persia.

All those Europeans who visited Isfahan between the middle sixties and the middle nineties of the last century were received in audience by the Zil and many of them have left an account of him. He was a stern and sometimes a savage despot who long remained in high favour in Tehran on account of the promptness with which he remitted to his father the taxes collected in the provinces in his charge. He professed the most liberal views and claimed to be an ardent Anglophile; he curbed the power of the *mullas*, kept the turbulent tribesmen in fair order, and suppressed brigandage. He built up the strength of his army, which was Prussian-trained and dressed in Prussian uniforms and *pickelhaubes*; the ' *links!* ', ' *rechts!* ' of the drill sergeants echoed over the Maidan, and the Zil was constantly having himself photographed in the full uniform of a Prussian general.

Dr Wills had the highest opinion of the Zil, whom he had treated after a gun accident; he thought he would make a bid for the throne when the time came, and that it would be ' a lucky day for Persia ' if he were to be successful. He considered the Vali-Ahd, on the other hand, to be half-witted, unstable, and a bigot. Curzon disagreed with him on both points. By the time Curzon reached Persia the Zil had already been stripped of almost all the provinces that till recently he had governed, and, when, in 1896, Nasir ad-din was assassinated, the Vali-Ahd ascended the throne without opposition from his brothers.

Curzon describes the Zil as short, corpulent and gouty, and with a defect in one eye. He rather doubted the sincerity of the Prince's Anglophile pretensions, for he had been heard to speak to Russians with equal enthusiasm for their country. After an interview with the Zil, Curzon wrote: ' Persia he depicted as " hungering and thirsting for civilization ", emotions of very dubious existence, which I question if the Zil would lift a finger to appease.' [110]

It was the greatest misfortune for Isfahan that the Zil conceived a hatred of everything Safavid. During his regime many of the Safavid buildings were allowed to fall into disrepair, and others were demolished. The difficulty of extracting money from Tehran for their preservation may in part have been responsible, but it does not provide a full explanation.

THE CHRISTIANS

When Lord Curzon visited Julfa seventy-five years ago, he reported that its inhabitants, by that time no more than 2,500 in number, fell roughly into four groups: (1) the Armenians proper, constituting the bulk of the community; (2) the United or Catholic Armenians—a small schism; (3) the Church of England Mission; and (4) the European mercantile and Telegraph element.

The Armenians proper were under the jurisdiction of an archbishop, who lived in a building, formerly a convent, adjoining the Cathedral. Attached to this was a nunnery of elderly spinsters who visited the sick, taught, and knitted socks, but whose annals ' had not been free from flagrant scandal.' Most of the younger generation emigrated to India, Java, and other places in the East, where they made good profits in business and lost all desire to return home. Those who remained were employed as market gardeners, carpenters and so on, and, in particular, in manufacturing liquor. This was partly for home consumption, but it was also sold at very lucrative prices on the sly to the Persians. Dr C. J. Wills, who lived in

Julfa for many years, wrote that his Armenian cook would say to him, ' Dinenr finished, Sir; if you no orders, I go get drunk with my priest.'

The Hamadan Armenian, though sometimes a drunkard, was in general hard-working and respectable; but, wrote Wills:

> The Isfahani looks upon the Julfa Armenian as a race apart, and merely the panderer to his vices and the maker of intoxicating liquors; and the hangdog Armenian with his sham Turk or European dress, and the bottle of arrack in his pocket, scowls staggering along in secure insolence, confident in the moral protection given him by the presence of the English whom he robs; respecting neither his priest, whom he has been taught to despise; nor the missionary whom he dislikes at heart [though he has educated his children gratuitously] and whom his priest openly reviles.[121]

The United or Catholic Armenians were a small schismatic group which origi-nated in 1688 when a Jesuit priest converted them to Rome. They built a church in 1705 and, after suffering the setbacks experienced by all Christian communities during the eighteenth century, were subsequently revived by the arrival of Catholic Armenians from India.

' The real jealousy, it is useless to deny,' wrote Curzon, ' is between the Arme-nians of both persuasions, and the Mission, sent out and supported by the Church of England Missionary Society, which has selected Julfa as the scene of an active propaganda and a large annual outlay.' The first Protestant missionary to come to Persia was the famous Henry Martyn, who arrived in Shiraz in 1811. Though no more than ' a beardless youth and evidently enfeebled by disease ' (of which he died the following year), he made a lasting impression by the charm of his perso-nality and his sheer goodness. A French Protestant, Eugène Boré, was in Isfahan in the 1830s, where he created much excitement and uproar by his preaching. Dr Bruce, of the Church Missionary Society, came to Julfa in 1869—' as good a type as can anywhere be seen of the nineteenth-century Crusader,' wrote Curzon. ' In an earlier age the red cross would have been upon his shoulder, and he would have been hewing infidels in conflict for the Holy Sepulchre, instead of translating the Bible, and teaching in schools at Julfa.' [122] Dr Bruce's converts were drawn ex-clusively from the members of the other Christian communities and not from among the Muslims. Curzon felt obliged to confess that he had never encountered a full-grown converted Muhammadan; Muhammadans had indeed been baptized, but they had invariably relapsed.

Canon Isaac Taylor, in an article entitled ' The Great Missionary Failure ' which appeared in the *Fortnightly Review* in 1888, wrote:

> In Persia, we are told that ' a great and wondrous door has been opened for the Gospel '; but no converts are mentioned, and the door seems to consist of a Persian who reads the Bible, which is one of his own sacred books. I have several correspondents among the Persian Moslems, and they continually quote the Bible, with which they seem to be almost as miliar as with the Koran.

Mrs Bishop (Isabella Bird) has exactly the same story to tell: ' The results (of Dr Bruce's proselytizing among Muslims), as results are usually estimated, are *nil*—that is, no Mohammedans openly confess Christianity.'

Certainly life was not easy for the Christians. In Curzon's day there was a promi-nent *Seyid*, or descendant of the Prophet, who spent his time fomenting anti-Christian riots in Isfahan. But Christian disunity was also in no small measure to blame for the lack of converts.

> Mussulmans [wrote Curzon] are perfectly entitled o scoff at those who invite them to enter a flock the different members of which love each other so bitterly. Protestants squabble with Roman Catholics, Presbyterians with Episcopalians, the Protestant Nestorians look with no very friendly eye upon the Nestorians proper, and these, again, are not on the most harmonious terms with the Chaldaeans, or Catholic Nestorians. The Armenians gaze askance upon the United [or Catholic] Armenians, and both unite in retarding the work of the Protestant missions. Finally, the hostility of the Jews may, as a rule, be reckoned upon. In the various countries of the East in which I

have travelled, from Syria to Japan, I have been struck by the strange and, to my mind, sorrowful phenomenon, of missionary bands waging the noblest of warfares under the banner of the King of Peace with fratricidal weapons in their hands.[123]

Today these feuds have died down. Isfahan is now the acknowledged preserve of the Church of England Missionary Society and the residence of the Protestant Bishop in Iran—at present an Iranian—and the mission hospital does invaluable and selfless work among people of all creeds, but the number of converts remains very small indeed.

Fig. 24. Tilework inscription from an Ivan of the Friday Mosque.

Part 5 The twentieth century

THE CONSTITUTIONAL REVOLUTION of 1905 almost unseated the precariously poised Qajar dynasty; at all events it considerably weakened the absolute power of the monarch.

In the First World War Iran declared her neutrality, but Tehran became a hotbed of intrigue for British, Russian and German agents and diplomats. The Turks marched on Tehran from Baghdad, but were defeated. In the south, 'Major (later General) Sir Percy Sykes recruited his South Persia Rifles and marched on Isfahan; on 11 September 1916 he entered the city, where a small Russian force had already arrived. A few days later a banquet, given by the Governor of Isfahan (the son of the Zil), was held in the Chihil Sutun.

After the Russian Revolution the Russian troops in Isfahan became completely demoralized. Drunken soldiers thieved and looted, and in the absence of proper patrolling their example was followed by Persian robbers and cut-throats who over-ran the surrounding country.

In 1922 came the final collapse of the Qajar dynasty and the seizure of power by Colonel Reza Khan of the Persian Cossack Brigade. In 1925, as Reza Shah, he became the first monarch of the Pahlevi dynasty. During the Second World War Iran again declared her neutrality and again became the centre of intrigue. In 1941 Reza Shah was obliged to abdicate; he was succeeded by his son, Muhammad Reza, the present Shah.

THE OPENING OF THE MOSQUES

Until about the year 1930, relatively few infidels had ever set foot within the mosques of Isfahan. 'They were known,' wrote Mr Christopher Sykes, only 'as enchanted views through doorways and no more ... They remained one of the most delicious and tempting speculations in the whole realm of architecture and decoration.' Then, suddenly, the doors began to be opened to western visitors.[124]

The British Consul-General in Isfahan at that time, Mr Ernest Bristow, had lived in Persia for nearly twenty years. He spoke Persian well and had many good friends among the Isfahanis. One of these was a man named Bahram—an engaging middle-aged Anglophile factotum and pimp, a soi-disant graduate of Balliol College, Oxford. Bristow asked Bahram whether, as Consul, he might be able to get permission to enter one or two of the more important mosques of Isfahan. The Persian replied that he had the ear of the Governor and was confident that the matter could be arranged.

Now the policy of Reza Shah was strongly anti-clerical, indeed anti-Islam; Bahram therefore, in approaching the Governor, employed the argument that Tehran would welcome the violation of the purity of the mosques by the feet of infidels. The Governor swallowed the bait, and Mr and Mrs Bristow were conducted into the Royal Mosque. Soon afterwards, two English aviators on a 'global' tour, Mrs Montague and Mr Belville, went with the Bristows to visit some of the principal mosques and thence with the report of their wonders to Tehran.

Mr Christopher Sykes, who was in Tehran at the time, wrote: ' It is no exaggeration to say that the news brought by the two English travellers was as if we had heard that the churches of the city of London were to be open to the public for the first time tomorrow.' Soon artists, archaeologists, and the idly curious began to arrive in Isfahan, and soon the facilities were extended to the other historical cities of Iran; thus the scientific study of Islamic architecture was inaugurated, eventually leading to the publication of Professor Upham Pope's monumental *Survey of Persian Art*, Robert Byron's *The Road to Oxiana*, and a host of other volumes of varying merit.[125]

With the fall of Reza Shah in 1941 and the subsequent recovery by the *mullas* of some of their lost power and prestige, the most sacred shrines of Iran, notably those of Meshed and Qum, once again became inaccessible. But in Isfahan the privileges once gained for Christian visitors were never again withdrawn; it is therefore to Isfahan that every student of Islamic architecture will first turn his steps today.

Anyone who compares the splendid photographs of the buildings of Isfahan in Professor Pope's *Survey*, with the buildings as they appear today, will see what fine work has been done to repair and conserve them. This is greatly to the credit of the Iranian Government, and also of their indefatigable French adviser, M. André Godard. Tile-work has been so superbly replaced that it is virtually impossible to distinguish old from new; who, for example, would ever guess that the whole of the tile-mosaic revetment of the portal of the Lutfullah Mosque is completely new? Yet Professor Pope's photograph shows this to be so.

This miracle of restoration is due in part to the skill of the craftsmen employed, who have used traditional methods of tile-making and cutting, but also to the fact that tiles, unlike stone, do not acquire a patina with age. Whatever restoration has been carried out in Iran has almost always been brilliantly done; unfortunately for every building that is saved, a dozen others are crumbling away for lack of money to preserve them.

ISFAHAN TODAY

Modern Tehran is a Western city with Oriental undertones. Meshed is still predominantly Oriental. In Isfahan the balance between East and West is still delicately maintained, though it is unlikely to remain so for much longer.

Oriental Isfahan is of course most easily sampled by the tourist in the bazaars, which are possibly the finest in all Asia. Though European dress is unfortunately becoming increasingly common, the atmosphere remains Oriental; the spirit of Hajji Baba, the hero of Morier's brilliant picaresque novel, still haunts the city, and there are still plenty of *chadors*, once-white baggy trousers, and turbans of several different colours to be seen.

The ever-beguiling feature of the bazaars is of course their endlessly varied kaleidoscope of sights and sounds and smells. Here are piles of pomegranates, of glittering pink candy, of sticky sweets, of curious spices. From some side alley comes the glimpse of a dye vat, with lengths of printed fabrics hung up to dry. In a courtyard, beside a blue-tiled pool, the shade of a pink-flowering almond tree falls upon the sleeping guardian of huge bales of improbable merchandise. There are the typical sounds: the strident hammering of the coppersmiths—so deafening that Chardin preferred to go a quarter of a league out of his way rather than endure it; the muffled hammering of the textile printers, the cries of the vendors, the bells of camels and of ancient bicycles, the indefinite throbbing sound of pullulating humanity.

There are the smells: the sickly smell of spices; the smell of leather and charcoal braziers and grilling meat, of cheese and oil; the rank odour of camel dung and of human sweat.

Such are the bazaars of Isfahan, and of many another Eastern city—Oriental indeed, but in themselves quite insufficient to give a proper picture of what life is like for half the population—the life that is carried on today almost exactly as it was in the time of Shah Abbas the Great and indeed long before his glorious reign.

In the bazaar area the alleys are narrow, pot-holed and stinking; they wind impossibly and defy the makers of street plans. Small children throw pebbles and pursue, jeering, the interloper from another world. The women, at the mere sight of a camera, vanish through ancient doorways into mysterious half-glimpsed courtyards. There are beggars with ugly sores; there is poverty—but no sign of starvation. This is the old Isfahan—the Isfahan that is now being swept away. A water system is under construction; a sewage system will follow. Broad new streets are being driven through the town, forming a grid which will eventually leave no ancient alley far from a tarmac road.

A typical feature of roads and pavements is the quantity of bric-à-brac that is strewn upon them. It is a common practice for carpet dealers to spread their new rugs in the middle of the streets, so that traffic passing over them will give them the appearance of age. Shoe-makers scatter the sunny pavements with shoes which will dry there more rapidly than in their shady booths; the presence of many other objects is difficult to account for. Yet in general there is little litter in the modern town, and the garden in the Maidan is kept spotless; only in the *jubs*—the water-channels that run beside the pavements of almost every street—is there refuse and stench.

There is still relatively little modern architecture in Isfahan, and nothing on a scale to dwarf the ancient buildings. The Bank Melli (National Bank) is a handsome contemporary building with little Iranian beyond its turquoise tiles. Several other banks and Government buildings, white and simple, do not seriously offend the eye.

The Maidan remains, of course, the focal point of Isfahan. Some will regret the passing, over a generation ago, of the wide open space of the polo ground, though the garden, with its welcome seats and flowers and pool, is charming enough. But all must deplore the giant modernistic light standards which have recently been erected; the concealed lighting in the arcading of the Maidan is, however, skilfully contrived, and produces an effect which must very closely resemble that obtained by the oil lamps used in the time of Shah Abbas for night festivals.

In the hour immediately before sunset the garden is usually full of peripatetic students, and the English or American visitor will often find himself politely approached for the meaning or correct pronunciation of an English word. Then, as the last rays of the setting sun gild the walls and flash upon the blue and honey-coloured domes, the lights are turned on and the students depart. It is suddenly night.

In Isfahan today it is the factory hooter, rather than the *muezzin*, which wakens the sleeping city; and as the minarets decay and fall, the factory chimneys rise. This does not mean that Islam is a dying force; far from it. There are *mullas* to be seen on every hand, and at the appointed hours of prayer the faithful, wherever they may be, perform without embarrassment the elaborate ritual enjoined by their creed. The *muezzin* can still be heard, though sometimes his voice will sound thin and weary, sometimes stridently amplified by the loudspeaker. But, as in many parts of Europe, it is principally the older generation, and especially the older women, who most resolutely cling to the consolation of religion. The *mullas*, by the reactionary attitude they have adopted over education and the emancipation of women, have lost favour with the young, who are determined to lead their own lives in their own way.

In the town itself, the principal mosques have become National Monuments where the stare of the tourist and the relentless click of his camera are not conducive to prayer. Here worshippers are few. The visitor who wishes to see the living Islam should go out on a Friday to (for example) the Imamzadeh Zain Abiyeh, which lies a mile or two to the north of the town. The court is thronged; the atmosphere is devout but informal. Kettles boil; the villagers picnic and gossip. The unbeliever is greeted cordially by the *mullas* and led into the shrine. Here he must remove his shoes, yet in the very sanctuary he will be offered a cigarette by the *mulla* himself: after all, what is fitting and what is sacrilegious in a sacred building are purely matters of convention.

Further evidence that Islam is still a living faith in Isfahan may be seen in the fine new mosque and *madraseh* which Colonel Zahedi is building, at his own expense, in the rapidly developing western quarter of the town. The design of the mosque is imaginative, combining traditional features with modern requirements. The tile-work shows that in this form of art the Iranian craftsman has lost little of his cunning.

The same may be said of carpet-making and textile-weaving, and the best Isfahan rugs are still fine examples of craftsmanship. The industry, which during the nineteenth century had languished, was revived after the First World War, and by 1935 there were some 2000 looms in the city and a further 500 or so in the surrounding villages. The designs were in general good, but the dyes poor and the pile cut too low; American buyers found the rugs too thin, and the demand for them came mainly from Europe. The Second World War nearly killed the industry; but the home market, and in particular the demand from Tehran, saved the situation. The present output, though much better in quality, is probably no more than half what it was forty years ago.

But the most important industry in Isfahan is that of spinning and weaving. New factories are rising on the southern bank of the Zayandeh-rud, and in private houses in many parts of the native city the sound of spinning and the click of the shuttle may be heard. The Shahnaz mills are the largest in Iran.

Besides the textile industry there is a large sugar mill and a cement factory. There are also, of course, the various trades that are carried on in the bazaars, for the bazaars are still workshops as well as shops. The silversmiths show incredible skill, and one cannot but be amazed by the ingenuity with which the workers in coarser metals contrive cauldrons and other vessels out of the most unpromising materials and with the simplest tools, or ornament coffers with the remnants of old metal containers and a few fragments of discarded velvet.

Though rug-making, weaving, and some of the lesser crafts are still flourishing in Isfahan, the fine arts are not. For the most part the painters of Isfahan today produce either tepid *rechauffés* of Safavid miniatures or 'Western' work of the kind that was fashionable in France before the First World War.

Those best qualified to judge speak highly of the literary revival in Iran, and especially in Tehran and Isfahan. Poetry is deeply engrained, still much quoted and still a living medium of expression. There are literary clubs in Isfahan, and in the courtyards behind some of the tea-houses of the Chahar Bagh the story-tellers are always surrounded by eager listeners.

The Isfahani, though he can always find time for the pleasures of the tea-house, has the reputation for industry. He is not by nature quarrelsome, and one rarely sees a street brawl or hears voices raised in anger. Less enviable is his reputation for tightfistedness, and the Shirazis, who spend money freely, allege that stinginess alone accounts for the slower development of the rival city.

Yet in this there is cause for thankfulness. Shiraz has lost much of its charm in its effort to become a second Tehran. Isfahan, guardian of the greatest collection of national monuments in all Iran, could so easily have been ruined in the cause of 'progress.' It is just because she has become something of a backwater, has been content to live on the heritage of her glorious past, that so relatively little of her beauty has perished. Had the Qajar or Pahlevi dynasties made her once more the capital city, Isfahan would have been ruined. There is another threat: Isfahan is rapidly developing its textile industry. Though one may certainly hope that it will prosper and increase, let us also hope that the pure air of Isfahan may never be polluted or her blue tiles blackened by industrial soot.

It is Isfahan's destiny to become the museum of Iran. As curiosity and the advances in air travel continually drive the tourist further afield, Iran will inevitably become a tourist country and Isfahan her greatest tourist attraction; one hopes that her charm will be preserved for all time. Few cities in the world have so much to offer the lover of—in the best sense of the word—the picturesque.

But the fate of Isfahan is bound up with the fate of Iran, and indeed with the fate of the whole Middle East. Though the Shah has attempted to break the power of the great land-owners, there is still much corruption in high places. Iran is at the cross-roads. Those who love her beautiful country and wonderful architecture, those who are truly grateful for the charm and kindness of her people, must fervently wish that she will find the solution to the many problems and difficulties that for many years to come must continue to beset her.

Short bibliography

Where there are a number of different editions of the work mentioned, the reference is usually made to that from which the quotation has been taken.

ABRAMOV, S., *see* MIKLUKHO-MAKLAI, N. D.

ALEXANDER A. SIGISMUNDO, Friar, *see Journal of the Royal Asiatic Society*, 1936, pp. 643 ff.

ANGIOLELLO, *see A Narrative of Italian Travels in Persia*. Hakluyt Society 1837.

ANON. *Hodud al-'Alam.*

ARBERRY, A. J. (ed.). *The Legacy of Persia*. Oxford 1935.

ATHAR-E-IRAN. *Annales du Service Archéologique de l'Iran*, vol. iv. 1949.

BARBARO, J. and CONTARINI, A. *Viaggi* (1543). Hakluyt Society 1873.

BASSET, J. *Persia*. 1887.

BELL, John. *Travels from St Petersburg...* 1874.

BELLAN, L. L. *Chah Abbas*, from *Les Grandes Figures de l'Orient*, vol. iii. 1932.

BINNING, R. B. *Travel in Persia*. 1857.

BISHOP, Mrs Isabella Bird. *Journeys in Persia*. 1891.

BLUNT, Wilfrid. *Pietro's Pilgrimage*. London 1953.
—. *A Persian Spring*. London 1957.

BODE, C. de. *Travels*. 1845.

BROWNE, E. G. *A Year amongst the Persians*. London 1893; Cambridge 1926.

BRUCE P. H. *Annals of the Honourable East India Company*, vol. iii. 1810.

BRUYN, C. de. *Travels*. 1737.

BUCKINGHAM, J. S. *Travels...* 1830.

BYRON, Robert. *The Road to Oxiana*. London 1937.

(CARMELITES). *A Chronicle of the Carmelites in Persia*. 1939.

CHARDIN, Sir J. *Voyages*. 1723.

CHEW, S. *The Crescent and the Rose*. New York 1937.

CLAIRAC, L-A. *Histoire de Perse*. 1750.

COSTE, P. *Monuments Modernes de la Perse*. 1867.

CURZON, Lord. *Persia*. 1892.

D'ALESSANDRI, *see A Narrative of Italian Travellers in Persia*. Hakluyt Society 1873.

DAULIER-DÉSLANDES, A. *Les Beautez de la Perse*. 1673.

DELLA VALLE, P. *Viaggi*. 1650.
—, *see* Blunt, W. *Pietro's Pilgrimage*. London 1953.

DIEULAFOY, J. *La Perse*. 1887.

DU CERCEAU, J. A. *The History of the Revolution of Persia*. 1728.

ELWELL-SUTTON, L. P. 'A Guide to Iranian Area Studies.' 1952.

FLANDIN, E. and COSTE, P. *Voyage en Perse*. 1851.
— — *Perse Moderne*. 1851.

FRASER, J. B. *Journey into Khorasan*. 1825.

FRY, R. N. *Iran*. 1954.

FRYER, J. *Travels* (1693). Hakluyt Society 1905-15.

GAIL, M. *Persia and the Victorians*. London 1951.

GILANENTZ, P. di S. *The Chronicle of Petros di Sarkis Gilanentz*, translated and annotated by Caro Minasian. Lisbon 1959.

GOVEA (GOUEVA), A. di. *Relation...* 1646.

GRAY, Basil. *Persian Painting*. 1961.

GROSECLOSE, E. *Introduction to Iran*. New York 1947.

GUIDE BLEU. *Moyen Orient*. Paris 1956.

HAMILTON, A. *A New Account of the East Indies*. 1727.

HANWAY, Jonas. *An Historical Account...* 1753.

HERBERT, Sir T. *Some Yeares Travaile*. 1634.

HONARFAR, L. *Historical Monuments of Isfahan*. 1964.

IBN ARABSHAH. *Timur the Great Amir*. London 1936.

IBN BATTUTA. *Travels in Asia and Africa, 1325-1354*. London 1929.

KAEMPFER, E. *Amoenitatum exoticarum... fasciculi*. 1712. This book deserves to be better known but unfortunately is not available in translation.

(KRUSINSKI, J. T.). *The Chronicles of a Traveller*. 1840.

LAMB, H. *Tamerlane, the Earth Shaker*. London 1929.

LOCKHART, L. *Nadir Shah*. London 1938.
— *Famous Cities of Iran*. London 1939.
— *The Fall of the Safavi Dynasty*. London 1958.

MALCOLM, Sir J. *History of Persia*. 1815.
— *Sketches of Persia*. 1815.

MIKLUKHO-MAKLAI, N. D. *Zapiski S. Avramova...* 1952.

MORIER, J. P. *Journey through Persia*. 1812.
— *Second Journey*. 1818.
— *Hajji Baba*. 1824-28.

NASIR-I-KHUSRAU. *Safar-Nameh*. Paris 1881.

OLEARIUS, A. *Travels*. 1669.

OUSELEY, Sir W. *Travels*. 1819.

PENROSE, Boies. *The Sherleian Odyssey*. 1938.

POPE, A. U. (ed.). *A Survey of Persian Art*. Oxford 1938.

PORTER, Sir R. K. *Travels*. 1821-22.

PRAWDIN, M. *The Mongol Empire*. London 1940.

SANSON, N. *The Present State of Persia*. 1695.

STACK, E. *Six Months in Persia*. 1882.

STEVENS, Sir R. *The Land of the Great Sophy*.

STRUYS, J. *Voiages and Travels*. 1684.

SYKES, Christopher. *Four Studies in Loyalty*. London 1946.

SYKES, Sir P. *A History of Persia*. London 1921.

TAVERNIER J. B. *The Six Voyages*. 1678.

TEXIER, Ch. *L'Arménie, la Perse...* 1842.

THEVENOT, J. *Travels*. 1687.

WILBER, D. N. *Iran: Past and Present*. Princeton 1948.
— *Architecture of Islamic Iran*. Princeton 1955.

WILSON, Sir A. *A Bibliography of Persia*. Oxford 1930.

Notes

[1] Blue, so dominant in Iranian tile-mosaic, is the celestial colour, the blue dome of the mosque being the microcosm imitating the macrocosm of the blue dome of the heavens.

[2] Quoted by Dr L. Honarfar, *Historical Monuments of Isfahan*, pp. 9-10.

[3] Adapted from Lockhart [1939], p. 15.

[4] The two principal sects of Islam [*see* p. 94].

[5] Ibn Battuta, p. 91.

[6] One authority states that Tamerlane sent a detachment of troops to protect the lives of scholars and priests.

[7] Ibn Arabshah, p. 45.

[8] Contarini, p. 131.

[9] *Uzun* means 'tall'.

[10] Pope, ii p. 1008 [Eric Schroeder].

[11] Niche directed towards Mecca.

[12] This style of decoration may also be studied in Hamadan, Ardistan, Yazd and Qazvin.

[13] In the nearby Jewish cemetery may be seen the tomb of Esther.

[14] Plate 363 B.

[15] Dieulafoy, p. 278.

[16] Curzon, ii, p. 58.

[17] Pope, ii, p. 1120.

[18] Pope, ii, pp. 1122-3 [Robert Byron].

[19] Pope, ii, p. 1331.

[20] Angiolello, p. 111.

[21] D'Alessandri, pp. 215-16.

[22] 'The Travels of a Merchant in Persia', in *A Narrative of Italian Travels in Persia* [Hakluyt Soc.], p. 165.

[23] Vol. ii, p. 1177.

[24] Mention may also be made of several other travellers who came to Isfahan in the seventeenth century:

Adam Olearius came to Persia in 1637 with an embassy from the Duke of Holstein, and remained in Isfahan for four or five months. Jean de Thévenot was a well-to-do, cultured Frenchman, a brilliant linguist and something of a botanist, who travalled, like Della Valle, in order to see the world. He spent the winter of 1664-5 in Isfahan, where he joined forces with Tavernier and set out for Indian. The Dutchman Jan Struys was in Isfahan in January 1672; there is as much of fantasy in his writing as in the engraving of the Royal Palace which illustrates the French edition [1681] of his Travels.

Sir John Chardin, a French Huguenot jeweller, came first to Persia in 1666 and later spent four years [1673-7] at the court of Shah Sulaiman-who employed him to purchase jewels. In 1681, because of the persecution of Protestants in France, he settled in England, where he was appointed court jeweller and was knighted by Charles II. Chardin's account of Isfahan is at once the most comprehensive and accurate of all those which describe the city under the Safavids.

Dr John Fryer, surgeon to the East India Company, published in 1698 the account of his nine years' travels, which took him to Isfahan in the summer of 1677. His style of writing is almost as comically engaging as that of Herbert. The last of the chroniclers who recorded Isfahan before its sack by the Afghans in 1722 was the Dutchman Cornelius de Bruyn, who [wrote Curzon] 'was always ready with his measuring rod and pencil, and while freely denouncing the errors of his predecessors, bequeathed a scarcely inferior stock for the critical delectation of his successors.'

[25] Carmelites, i, p. 104.

[26] Carmelites, i, p. 285 ff. Father John was made first Bishop of Isfahan in 1632.

[27] Carmelites, i, p. 169.

[28] Carmelites, i, pp. 287-8.

[29] Some doubt exists as to the precise years in which work was started on some of these buildings. Lockhart states that the Royal Mosque was begun in 1590, and the Chihil Sutun at the close of the sixteenth century.

[30] A few years ago the authorities planned to build large blocks of flats in the centre of the Maidan. M. Godard, the French Director of Antiquities in Iran at the time, prevented this enormity, and the municipal garden was a compromise.

[31] Even this was presumably removed when polo was played.

[32] Herbert, pp. 128 and 129.

[33] Tavernier, i, p. 152.

[34] ii, pp. 295-301.

[35] *Sketches*, Chapter 5.

[36] The *talar* is one of the most ancient of Persian architectural traditions, dating back at least to the Hall of a Hundred Columns at Persepolis. These little palaces fronted by a *talar* are often called *Kolah Farangi*—'Franks' Hats'—by the Persians.

[37] ii, p. 80.

[38] ii, p. 39.

[39] *The Road to Oxiana*, pp. 176-8.

[40] There seems to be some doubt as to the date when work actually began on the Mosque. Mme Dieulafoy wrote: '*La première pierre... fut*

posée en 1580. *A date de ce jour, les travaux marchèrent avec une fiévreuse activité.*' Lockhart says, ' begun in 1590, partly finished in 1616, and completed in 1640.' That work on the Mosque itself had not advanced very far by 1617 seems to be suggested by Della Valle's letter of that year, in which he states that ' the foundations have been laid, and they are at work embellishing the building...' I have accepted the dates most usually given [*see also* Pope, ii, p. 1188].

41 There was a brief period in the 1930s when Reza Shah, as a part of his campaign to curtail the power of the *mullas*, allowed Christians access to many of the most sacred shrines in Iran. *See* p. 196.

42 Vol. vi, p. 306.

43 Vol. vi, pp. 287-8.

44 Vol. vi, p. 184.

45 Vol. vi, p. 186.

46 Vol. vi, pp. 187-8.

47 Vol. vi, pp. 20-21.

48 For a clear and succinct account of Sunnism and Shi'ism *see* Stevens, pp. 39-45.

49 Tavernier, i, pp. 161-3. Della Valle, de Bruyn and Thévenot are among other writers who describe the Festival of Husain.

50 The quotations from Della Valle, here and elsewhere, are taken from the author's *Pietro's Pilgrimage* [James Barrie, 1953].

51 Herbert, p. 122.

52 Copies of the inscriptions on many of these are in the Museum attached to the Cathedral.

53 *See* Tavernier, i, pp. 207-9 and Olearius, i, pp. 505-7. The two accounts vary in detail.

54 Carmelites, i, pp. 93-4.

55 ' If it were the practice of Abbas to sit on the ground, knees in front, heels tucked under him... this would not have meant any particular act of homage or respect, beyond that mark of politeness in offering the cup with his own hand.' [Carmelites, i, p. 91].

56 Carmelites, i, p. 91. Report furnished by the Carmelite Fr Paul Simon of Jesus Mary.

57 *See* Carmelites, i, pp. 104 ff.

58 The manuscript was described by Sir Sydney Cockerell in 1927. Its history is interesting. After passing from Paris to Naples, at the beginning of the seventeeth century it came into the possession of a Polish Cardinal who presented it in 1608 to Shah Abbas. Sold at some later date by an Arab to a Greek for three shillings, it was sent by the latter to Sotheby's in 1833, where it was purchased by a firm of booksellers, Payne and Foss, for 255 guineas. Next it passed into the hands of that omniverous bibliophile and collector, Sir Thomas Phillips, and finally, by private purchase, to John Pierpont Morgan. Since the Carmelites had passed through Poland, it is not unreasonable to assume that they had brought the manuscript with them.

59 Carmelites, ii, p. 1032.

60 Carmelites, ii, p. 1039.

61 Carmelites, ii, p. 1035.

62 Pp. 384-7.

63 Bruce, iii, p. 315.

64 The advantage of a treaty over the more usual agreement [*raqam*] was that it did not need renewal [involving further gifts and bribes] upon the death of a monarch.

65 *See* Lockhart [1958], pp. 437-72.

66 Fryer [vol. ii, pp. 309-11] gives a list of the flowers, fruit and vegetables grown.

67 i. pp. 576-7.

68 His real name was Sam, but Abbas ordered that the should assume the name of his late father.

69 Carmelites, ii, p. 308. Father John Thaddeus, writing in 1629, adds the following curious detail: ' This King has not yet been circumcised; and, when the notables pressed him to be, he made excuses, saying he was too old and could not bear such great pain.'

70 Jesuit and historian, *see* p. 153.

71 Vol. ii, p. 33.

72 i, pp. 582-3.

73 *See* Carmelites, ii, p. 405.

74 P. 6.

75 Carmelites, ii, pp. 35 and 45-7.

76 Persian mystics.

77 i, pp. 104-5.

78 Quoted in Carmelites, ii, p. 472.

79 For Farahabad *see* Pope, ii, 1434-6.

80 It is also possible that the Imarat Bihisht was the palace destroyed by Sultan Husain [*see* p. 144].

81 I am grateful to Mr David Blow for drawing my attention to these portraits.

82 Tavernier, i, pp. 181 ff. and Daulier-Déslandes, pp. 17 ff.

83 Carmelites, ii, pp. 557-8.

84 There were in fact only *seven* paradises. This name was sometimes given to eight-sided pavilions and entrance lodges.

85 P. 249.

86 Curzon [i, p. 340] says that the Shah himself composed an ode in Strachey's honour, and that the portrait of Strachey in the Kasr-i-Qajar was hung ' between the mythic heroes, Zal and Afrasiab—an apotheosis which I am not aware that any other Englishman has ever attained.'

87 Quoted and translated by Curzon, ii, p. 37.

88 Vol. 1, p. 200.

[89] For a description and photograph of these, *see Athar-e-Iran*, Tome II, Fasc. i, 1937.

[90] For the invasion *see* Clairac, Gilanentz, Krusinski, Lockhart [1958] and Sykes. The accounts vary in detail, but both are substantially the same.

[91] *See* Sykes, ii, pp. 216-30.

[92] Now a part of the large village of Sehdeh [Lockhart].

[93] Krusinski, ii, p. 123.

[94] A reliable estimate of the number who died during the siege is about 100,000. This is probably about three times the number of those who died in battle.

[95] Joseph Apisalaimian, the French Consul's Armenian interpreter, was present and his account was used by Louis-André de Clairac in the latter's *Histoire de Perse*.

[96] ii, pp. 159-60.

[97] Muhammad Quli Khan, who had helped Afghans in Qazvin to escape the fury of the mob.

[98] R.C.J.A. vol. xxiii, part IV, p. 651 [quoted by Lockhart].

[99] Vol. ii, p. 16.

[100] So-called because it was written in red ink [Lockhart].

[101] ii, p. 152.

[102] ii, p. 237.

[103] ii, p. 165.

[104] *See* Lockhart [1958] for a full and brilliant account.

[105] His account was published in Russian, but see extracts given by Lockhart [1958], pp. 313-20.

[106] *See* p. 150.

[107] ii, p. 244.

[108] *See* Lockhart, L., *Nadir Shah*, 1938.

[109] Carmelites, i, p. 649.

[110] William Cockell, in James Fraser's *The History of Nadir Shah*, p. 227.

[111] *Don Juan*, Canto No. IX, xxxiii. A footnote in the 1833 edition states that Nadir's temper ' had been exasperated by his extreme costiveness to a degree of insanity.'

[112] So wrote Chardin, a reliable witness who knew London well. London was at that time the largest city in Europe, with a population of about 670,000 inhabitants.

[113] Carmelites, i, p. 707.

[114] P. 134.

[115] P. 135.

[116] P. 136.

[117] Pp. 144-51.

[118] Other nineteenth-century works containing useful information about Isfahan include those of J. S. Buckingham, J. Baillie Fraser, E. Stack and Mrs Bishop. Of great but more general interest is E. G. Browne's *A Year amongst the Persians* [1893, new edition 1926].

[119] Two had died in infancy.

[120] i, pp. 419-20.

[121] Quoted by Curzon, ii, p. 53.

[122] ii, p. 56.

[123] i, p. 507.

[124] The circumstances which brought about this change of heart have been delightfully described by Mr Christopher Sykes in the second of his *Four Studies in Loyalty*, ' The Inspiration of a Persian.'

[125] Sir Roger Stevens' *The Land of the Great Sophy*, Dr Laurence Lockhart's *Famous Cities of Iran* and *Moyen Orient* [Guide Bleu] are indispensable companions for all who visit Iran today.

Index